بسم الله الرحمن الرحيم

In the name of God, most Gracious, most Merciful

The Importance of Sisterhood in Islam

according to the Qur'an and the Sunnah

Ruqaiyah Abdullah

Ta-Ha Publishers
1 Wynne Road
London SW9 0BB
UK

Copyright © Ruqaiyah Abdullah

Published Rajab 1421/October 2000 by:
Ta-Ha Publishers Ltd.
1 Wynne Road
London SW9 0BB
website: http://www.taha.co.uk
email: sales@taha.co.uk

All rights reserved. No part of this publication may be reproduced, stored in any retrieval system, or transmitted in any form or by any means, electronic or otherwise, without written permission of the publishers.

By: Ruqaiyah Abdullah
Edited by: Abdassamad Clarke
General Editor: Afsar Siddiqui

A catalogue record for this book is available from the British Library.

ISBN 1 84200 01 7 9
Typeset by: Bookwright
website: http://www.bogvaerker.dk/Bookwright
email: Bookwright@bogvaerker.dk

Printed and bound by: Deluxe Printers, London.
website: http://www.de-luxe.com
email: de-luxe@Talk21.com

Bismillahir Rahmanir Raheem

Preface

All praise is due to Allah. We praise Him, we seek His aid and we ask for His forgiveness. We seek Allah's refuge from the evils of ourselves and the evils of our actions. Whomsoever Allah guides, there is no one to misguide him and whomsoever Allah misguides, there is no one to guide him. I testify that none has the right to be worshipped except Allah alone, Who has no partner and I testify that Muhammad is His slave and Messenger (saas).

Has community spirit become a thing of the past? Or is it possible to revive the concept of sisterhood in Islam?

The Muslim community should be a strong cohesive body, united by universal ties of brotherhood/sisterhood. The teachings of brotherhood are clear in the Qur'an and the Sunnah of the Prophet (SAAS), and it is the duty of every Muslim to abide by these teachings to ensure a harmoniously balanced and proper functioning society. If we fail to adhere to these teachings and instead act according to our own emotional feelings and desires, dissension and division will be inevitable.

In Islam, there is a strong emphasis on maintaining good relations with family and community members, irrespective of whether they are Muslim or non-Muslim. The virtues of patience, tolerance and understanding, forgiveness, mutual kindness, sympathy and concern are all qualities of a good practising Muslim. Good manners and behaviour are also meritorious qualities reflecting iman and taqwa. Muslim women have certain rights, duties and responsiblilities towards their fellow sisters-in-Islam. These rights and obligations should be honoured at all times. If we fail to uphold these rights, we will not only fail to fulfil our duty towards Allah (SWT) and towards our fellow Muslim sisters, but we will also fail to reap benefits and rewards for ourselves in this life and the Next.

This book aims to explore the rewards for fulfilling our Islamic duties and obligations and the punishment for certain failings in our everyday social responsibilities. It will also mention how certain actions and behaviour have a detrimental effect on ties of sisterhood in the Muslim Ummah (community). It will also provide Islamic advice and guidance for correcting our behaviour according to the Qur'an and Sunnah of the Prophet (SAAS).

I hope Allah (SWT) accepts my humble efforts and forgives me for any errors I may have made. May Allah (SWT) continue to send peace and blessings upon the Prophet (SAAS) and guide us all towards strengthening the Muslim Ummah (ameen).

Abbreviations and Arabic Terms

This book contains the following abbreviations and Arabic terms:

SWT	–	*subhanahu wa ta'ala* (glorious is He and exalted)
SAAS	–	*sall'Allahu 'alaihi wa sallam* (may Allah bless him and grant him peace)
RA	–	*radiy'Allahu 'anhu* (may Allah be pleased with him)
		radiy'Allahu 'anha (may Allah be pleased with her)
		radiy'Allahu 'anhum (may Allah be pleased with them)
AS	–	*'alaihi's-salam* (peace be upon him)
		'alaihimu's-salam (peace be upon them)

Arabic terminology

adab	–	courtesy
ayat	–	sing. ayah. Verses of the Qur'an
bid'ah	–	innovation
deen	–	the life-transaction of Islam, iman and ihsan
hadith	–	pl. ahadith. Saying or account of an action of the Prophet Muhammad (SAAS)
iman	–	True faith consisting of belief in the heart, speech on the tongue and action of the limbs
kuffar	–	Those who cover over the truth
mumin	–	pl. muminun. Those who have iman.
sunnah	–	the custom and practice of the Prophet (SAAS)
taqwa	–	fearful awareness of Allah resulting in the performance of His obligations and avoidance of His prohibitions

Contents

Preface		iv
Introduction		1
1.	True Sisters in Islam	2
	Sisterhood and Muslim Unity	2
	Culture and Islam	3
	Race Relations in Islam	5
	Keeping Good Company	10
2.	Spiritual Obligations toward Fellow Sisters	13
	A Compassionate Community	13
	Encouraging One Another in Iman	14
	Praying with Sisters in Congregation	16
	Remembering Sisters in Supplications	18
3.	Attitude and Behaviour toward Fellow Sisters	19
	Good Manners	19
	Love for Fellow Sisters	21
4.	The Rights of a Sister over Another Sister	24
	Meeting and Greeting Sisters	26
	Celebrations and Conveying Glad Tidings	29
	Visiting Muslim Women and Guests	32
	Generosity	33
	Giving and Receiving Gifts	34
	Adab in Social Gatherings	35

	Entertaining Sisters and Guests	36
	Adab of Eating	37
	Adab of Serving Drinks	43
	Invoking Blessings upon Someone who Sneezes	44
	Visiting the Sick	45
5.	Adab in Speech	47
	Honesty in Speech	48
	Whispering and Private Conversations	50
	Tact and Discretion	51
	Keeping Secrets	52
	Gossip and Idle Talk	54
	Backbiting	57
	Slander	59
	Seeking Forgiveness for Backbiting and Slander	61
	Concealing Faults	62
	Being Two Faced	65
	Envy	66
	Quarrelling	67
	Controlling Anger	71
	Cutting Ties with Sisters	72
6.	Conclusion	75

Introduction

Sisterhood is a very important aspect of Islam, yet its true significance is often under-valued. Sisterhood entails many rights and responsibilities, and mutual duties and obligations. Despite this, it is disappointing to see how little of it we actually observe and put into practice. This raises several important questions. Why are we not fulfilling our Islamic obligations towards other Muslim women? Is it because we do not know what they are, or are there certain barriers that hinder us from fulfilling them? Are we lazy, ignorant or merely incapable of observing these simple acts of sisterhood? Or do we allow negative emotions, grudges, prejudice and intolerance to dictate the way we think and behave towards one another? Whatever the reasons may be or the excuses we may give, we should not harbour ill feelings as they will make us more negative, intolerant and resistant to change. Instead we should acknowledge our personal difficulties and weaknesses, and find effective ways of overcoming them. This will help us to break down social barriers that hinder Muslim unity and to move closer towards strengthening and maintaining strong ties among Muslim women in the community.

Throughout this book we will explore different aspects of Islamic sisterhood and the rewards and benefits for fulfilling our social duties and obligations. Similarly we will highlight the problems that may occur if we neglect or forget to fulfill these duties, and mention some of the punishments that we may incur in this life and the next. Supporting evidence is taken from ayahs of the Qur'an and from the Sunnah of the Prophet Muhammad (SAAS).

True Sisters in Islam

Sisterhood and Muslim Unity

Sisterhood is vital for strengthening community ties and preserving iman and identity. Moreover, it is important for Muslims to have a genuine sense of belonging, and to share sincere mutual love and concern for one another. Unfortunately, the true essence of sisterhood has been eroded by the negative influence of weak Muslims and non-Muslims who are ignorant of Islamic values and social moral Adab (courtesy). Instead they adopt anti-social attitudes and behaviours from life in jahiliyyah (pre-Islamic ignorance). Some of these behaviours include suspicion, backbiting, gossiping, verbal and physical abuse, racism and ostracism, all of which have contributed towards disharmony and disunity between Muslims.

Some Muslim women have broken away from the main body of Islam to form distinct separate groups. Some of these partisan groups form due to a difference in Islamic knowledge or opinion, while others form on the pretext of Islam to conceal other hidden agendas. Some of these groups form on the basis of shared common features or attributes such as nationality, race, language or skin colour, while others form because of a shared interest or common cause such as political and environmental issues, employment, sport, support groups and so on. Unfortunately these worldly causes fail to satisfy the needs and interests of all mankind and cannot therefore unite people universally. In many cases they create further tension and division.

Islam however universally binds the people of iman through spiritual unification by means of peace and mutual co-operation. Islam is a complete way of life that satisfies every basic human need and requirement. It shapes social norms and values and provides correct guidance for social, moral attitude and conduct. Allah (SWT) provides His Guidance to help regulate social behaviour and form close, successful relationships with our fellow men, or in our case – fellow women. The word for human being in Arabic does not prefer male over female but refers to both. This guidance is clear in the Qur'an and the Sunnah of the Prophet Muhammad (SAAS). If we adhere to this guidance, we are in fact worshipping and obeying Allah (SWT), and ensuring a better position in this life and the Next, insha'Allah.

This nation of yours is one nation and I am your Lord, so worship Me. (Surat al-Anbiya: 91)

Culture and Islam

Culture is the term used to describe the unity of a group by 'their way of life,' shared values, norms, customs and habits. This includes dress codes, marriage rites, patterns of work, festivals and ceremonies, leisure activities, eating habits and so on. When we adopt similar social attitudes and patterns of behaviour it helps create familiarity and maintain good relations with other members in the group.

However, culture is not universal. Norms and values of behaviour are extremely diverse and can vary greatly from one culture to another. They can even vary within the same culture to thus form sub-cultures. When we differ in opinion from what is considered 'normal,' 'acceptable' or 'correct' standards of behaviour we become opposed and divided from one another. This is why man requires universal guidance that is infallible and remains consistent over time, rather than one that is often open to debate or subject to change.

Islam is revealed by Allah (SWT) to correct and perfect the noble qualities of character and social moral guidance for all of mankind and is far superior to other religions and man-made theories and ideologies. It provides a universal 'way of life,' which unites all believing men and women from every nation, worldwide. The whole essence of Islam is based upon peace and harmony and instils the idea of a shared socialisation rather than selfish individualism. Each individual is a member of the wider community and shares responsibility for the spiritual and socio-economic welfare of its other members.

Allah (SWT) revealed His guidance for the benefit of society as a whole, yet many people still prefer to follow the ways of their family ancestors. Many Muslims place more importance on culture than Islam and pride themselves on ancestry and family tradition. Muslims who blindly follow the ways of their cultural forefathers are in danger of committing *shirk* (associating others in worship with Allah). This is because they prefer to fulfill cultural expectations to please their own family members rather than fulfill Islamic obligations to gain the Pleasure of Allah (SWT).

There are many hidden dangers in giving preference to culture over Islam. Muslims may begin to rely more upon innovations (*bid'ah*) than authentic Islamic knowledge and break away from the main body of Islam. They are then more likely to invent their own peculiar ways of practising or expressing their faith. The Prophet (SAAS) warned that the Muslims will divide into seventy-three sects, but only one will enter the Garden. This group is the one who follows the Qur'an and the Sunnah of the Prophet Muhammad (SAAS). It is therefore important for us to unite together on this rightly guided path and invite other Muslim women to do the same:

> The Jews and the Christians divided into seventy-one or seventy-two sects, and this nation will divide itself into seventy-three sects – all in the Fire, except one, and that one is the one which I and my companions are on today (i.e. following the Qur'an and the Sunnah – practice of the Prophet SAAS). (Abu Hurairah (RA) in Abu Dawud. Vol. III, p 1291, No. 4579 up to the words "seventh-three sects", and the second half 'Abdullah ibn 'Amr (RA) in at-Tirmidhi, 0171. Also Ibn Majah)

Some Muslim sisters are better influences on us than blood-related sisters. This is because they may encourage us to strive more for the Hereafter than the life of this world and advise us according to authentic Islamic knowledge, rather than innovations (*bid'ah*) and misguidance. In the Qur'an, Allah (SWT) warns about the dangers of being led astray by family members. He illustrates the point with particular reference to the family members of previous prophets. We already know that the wives of Nuh [Noah] and Lut [Lot], and the father of Ibrahim [Abraham] (AS) are destined for the Fire for failing to have iman.

> **When they are told, 'Follow what Allah has sent down to you,' They say, 'We are following what we found our fathers doing.' What, even though their fathers did not understand a thing and were not guided! (Surat al-Baqarah 2: 169)**

&

When they are told: 'Follow what Allah has sent down,' they

say, 'No, we will follow what we found our fathers doing.' What! Even if Shaytan is calling them to the punishment of the Blazing Fire? (Surah Luqman 31: 20)

Ancestral pride is a wrong action worthy of punishment in the Fire. The Prophet (SAAS) warned us not to indulge in ancestral pride, as this was the custom in pre-Islamic time. Instead man is considered honourable in Allah's eyes (SWT) only by his iman and right actions.

> Allah Most High, has removed from you the pride of the pre-Islamic period and its boasting of ancestors. One is only a pious mumin or a miserable wrongdoer. You are sons of Adam, and Adam came from dust. Let the people cease to boast about their ancestors. They are merely fuel for Jahannam; or they will certainly be of less account with Allah than the beetle which rolls dung with its nose. (Abu Hurairah (RA) in Abu Dawud, Vol. III, p1418, No. 5097)

Race Relations in Islam

Allah (SWT) gave man superiority over all creation including the angels, animals and jinn. When He created Adam from wet sounding clay, He breathed life (his *ruh*) into him and ordered the angels and jinn to bow down before him. Shaytan was a jinn, who refused to prostrate before Adam, because he believed Adam was created inferior to him. Shaytan was created from smokeless fire, while Adam was created from clay. Allah (SWT) ordered that Shaytan be punished in the Fire for his arrogance, jealousy, and disobedience, but the punishment is deferred to the Last Day. This heinous crime was, in one way, similar to racism. By analogy, Allah (SWT) warns us if people adopt this attitude by declaring themeslves superior in terms of nationality, race or skin colour, they will also find their final abode in the Fire.

> When your Lord said to the angels, 'I am creating a human being out of dried clay formed from fetid black mud. When I have formed him and breathed My Ruh into him, fall down in prostration in front of him!' (Surat al-Hijr 15: 28-29)

Some use the English translation of the ayat above to justify and legitimise their claim to superiority over other Muslims in terms of race and colour. This is because their interpretation of the translation implies that Adam was black and they then go on to allege that it was because of his skin colour that Allah (SWT) ordered His creation to prostrate before him. However, Allah (SWT) created Adam from a handful of clay taken from all over the earth. Hence the children of Adam are according to the soil: some red, some white, some black, some a mixture, some are smooth and rough, some are bad and some are good. (Abu Musa al-Ash'ari (RA) in Abu Dawud, Vol. III, p1314, No. 4676) Despite this, a black political organisation called the Nation of Islam use this ayat to attract new members. Although the Nation of Islam believe in 'La illaha illa Allah – There is no God but Allah,' they do not believe that the Prophet Muhammad (SAW) was the final messenger and seal of all the prophets. Instead they believe that other men have become prophets after the time of the Prophet Muhammad (SAW). This takes them out of the fold of Islam for failing to acknowledge the first condition of the kalimah. (See Surat al-Ma'idah 5:3). They use the name of Islam to address race issues, and twist its doctrines to help redress the balance of power between black and white. Their main aim is to eliminate racial discrimination, prejudice and oppression, and elevate the status and position of black people rather than further the cause of Islam. Ironically, the rationale behind the Nation of Islam is itself racist, as they only appeal to the needs and interests of one nation, namely the black community. Islam should not be used as a political platform to further the interests of one particular group, since Islam exists to serve the interests of people of all nations.

Some Arab Muslims assume they have some superiority over other Muslims because they speak the language of the Qur'an, i.e. Arabic. However, Allah (SWT) is the Only One, who has the Power to judge the different degrees of the Muslims, which are according to their level of iman and right actions. This, of course, varies from individual to individual. Some people assume that white British reverts are stronger and more sincere in the Deen than other Muslims. Once again, this is a misconception, as strength and sincerity of iman also vary from person to person. Allah (SWT) judges a white British revert on the same basis as any other Muslim, whether he is black, Asian, Chinese, American, German or Egyptian.

> There is no superiority for an Arab over a non-Arab or a non-Arab over an Arab or a white person over a black or a black person over a white, except through taqwa. (Ahmad)

Similarly, some Muslims born and raised in Islam believe they are superior to those who reverted to the Deen. They assume that because they have been Muslims all their lives they have greater Islamic knowledge. Once again, this is not necessarily the case. Despite being Muslims for fewer years, some reverts may have better Islamic knowledge than people who have been born Muslims, or they may have less knowledge but practise fewer innovations (bid'ah). Some Muslims assume that the Garden is ultimately a birthright. However, Muslims will only be granted entry into the Garden if they have sincere iman in Allah (SWT) and hold the correct tenets of Islam, and not merely just pay lip service to them. Ancestral arrogance and pride can be particularly dangerous, as they can make us critical of other Muslims and self complacent in our own Islamic practice. Allah (SWT) warns of the punishment for hypocrites who fail to practise what they preach in the following ayat:

> **Among the people there are some who say, 'We have iman in Allah and the Last Day,' when they are not muminun... They will have a painful punishment on account of their denial. (Surat al-Baqarah 2 : 8-10)**

&

> A man will be brought and put in the Fire and he will circumambulate in the Fire like the donkey in a flour-mill, and all the people of the Fire will gather around him and will say to him: "O so and so! Didn't you use to order others to do *ma'ruf* (tawhid and all that is good) and forbid them from *munkar* (assocation of partners with Allah, disbelief and all that is evil)?" That man will say, "I used to order others to do *mar'uf* but I never used to do it, and I used to forbid others doing *munkar* while I myself used to do it." (Abu Wa'il (RA), al-Bukhari, Vol. 9, p170, No. 218)

Allah (SWT) forbids us looking down upon fellow Muslims, or belittling them because of our own cultural arrogance and self pride:

> **You who have iman! people should not ridicule others who may be better than themselves; nor should any women ridicule other women who may be better than themselves. And do not find fault with one another or insult each other with derogatory nicknames. How evil it is to have a name for evil conduct after coming to iman! Those people who do not turn from it are wrongdoers. (Surat al-Hujurat 49: 11)**

We all belong to Allah (SWT), and our final return is to Him. We are all created in the same way and for the same purpose, which is to worship and obey One God, Allah (SWT). We originate from the same source (Adam and Hawa) and are all united in a universal brotherhood of Islam. We may differ in colour, language, build or feature, but these are not expressions of superiority or inferiority, they merely express the natural diversity of mankind.

> **Among His Signs is that He created you from dust and here you are now, widespread human beings! (Surat ar-Rum 30:19)**
>
> &
>
> **Among His Signs is the creation of the heavens and the earth and the variety of your languages and colours. There are certainly Signs in that for every being. (Surat ar-Rum 30:22)**

Allah (SWT) created us in different nations, races and tribes so that we might come to know one another and learn to accept and respect our similarities and differences. These distinctions and diversities in human nature do not exist to create enmity and hostility. Instead they bring variety and interest to many aspects of everyday life. Despite this, some people use nationality or skin colour as criteria for measuring human worth in order to exert superiority over others. The criterion for measuring a person's worth is not the colour of his skin, his race, or social standing. Instead, Allah (SWT) judges us individually, according to our iman and right actions. In Islam, the concept of a 'chosen' or 'superior' race or nation does not exist. Allah (SWT) sent prophets to previous generations with specific missions to their own peoples. However the Prophet Muhammad (SAAS) was sent to spread the message of Islam to people of all nations. Islam is the only true religion that aims to bridge the gap between individuals and groups and thus encourages good relations between peoples:

> **Mankind! We created you from a male and female, and made you into peoples and tribes so that you might come to know each other. The noblest among you in Allah's sight is the one with the most taqwa. Allah is All-Knowing, All-Aware. (Surat al-Hujurat 49: 13)**
>
> **We have only sent you (Muhammad) as a mercy to all the**

worlds. (Surat al-Anbiya 21: 107)

Muslims are united in their iman in Allah, and in their means of worshipping Him (Allah SWT). Iman strengthens community ties and joins nations together. This is why Allah (SWT) commands us to maintain Muslim solidarity by uniting in the one true deen – Islamic *tawhid*.

Hold fast to the rope of Allah all together, and do not separate. (Surah Al 'Imran 3: 103)

If a Muslim breaks away from the main body of Islam due to cultural arrogance, ancestral pride or due to a difference of opinion in the deen, then he has gone astray, especially if the difference in opinion involves error or innovation. The punishment for abandoning the consensus of the Muslims is the Fire. The following hadiths re-iterate these points:

Who ever separates from the community (the Muslim Ummah) – even a span – has removed the rope of Islam from his neck. (Abu Dharr (RA), Abu Dawud, p1332, No. 4740)

&

Surely Shaytan is like a wolf to man. Just as the wolf attacks the sheep that strays away from the flock, wanders and goes to a corner, Shaytan attacks the person who separates himself from the Muslim community. So avoid the various sects and stick to the united body. (Mu'adh ibn Jabal (RA), Ahmad)

&

Allah will not allow my followers to agree on a matter involving error, and remember that the hand and mercy of Allah is with the united body. Whoever separates himself from it will be separated (from the Muslim Ummah and) enter the Fire. ('Umar ibn al-Khattab (RA), at-Tirmidhi)

&

One who defects from obedience (to the amir) and separates from the main body of the Muslims – if he dies in that state – will die the death of one belonging to the days of Jahiliyyah (i.e. would not die as a Muslim). (Abu Hurairah (RA), Muslim)

Keeping Good Company

Sisterhood is important in Islam. It has vast significance and meaning and encompasses a wide range of principles and practices. However the true essence of sisterhood can only be understood and preserved if we all adhere to the correct Islamic teachings, and remain in the company of other like-minded Muslim women. If we associate with Muslim women who are weak and act according to their desires and emotions rather than obeying Allah's guidance we may be influenced to do the same. The Muslim Ummah is then likely to fall further into disunity. The Prophet (SAAS) emphasised the importance of keeping good company and used the following analogy to explain the difference between good and bad friends:

> The similitude of good company and that of bad company is that of the owner of musk and the ironsmith and his bellows. The owner of musk would either offer you it free of charge or you would buy it from him or you would smell its pleasant odour. As for the ironsmith blowing his bellows, he would either burn your clothes or you will have to smell its repugnant smell. (Abu Musa (RA), Muslim, Vol IV, p201, No. 2628)

&

> A person follows the deen of his close friend, therefore let each of you look carefully at whom he chooses for friends. (Abu Hurairah (RA), Abu Dawud, Vol. III p1350, No. 4815. At-Tirmidhi. *Riyad as-Salihin*, Vol. I, p161, No. 367)

The Prophet (SAAS) warned that the worst company is those who disbelieve in Allah (SWT), and those who do not remember Him or follow His divine laws and guidance. Instead they choose to believe in man-made theories and belief systems and are misguided far from the Truth. If we obey the laws of man before the laws of our Creator, we will be among the losers in this life and the next:

If you obeyed most of those on earth, they would misguide you from Allah's Way. They follow nothing but conjecture. They are only guessing. (Surat al-An'am 6 : 116)

&

> People who get up from an assembly in which they did not remember Allah will be just as if they had got up from an ass's

corpse, and it will be a cause of grief to them. (Abu Hurairah (RA), Abu Dawud, p1354. No. 4837)

&

If anyone sits in a place where he does not remember Allah, deprivation will descend on him from Allah; and if he lies in a place where he does not remember Allah, deprivation will descend on him from Allah. (Abu Hurairah (RA), Abu Dawud, Vol. III, p1355, No. 4838 & Vol. III, p1404, No. 5041)

The Prophet (SAAS) also warned Muslims not to keep close company of Jews, Christians and pagans, as they may advise them badly or lead them astray. If we prefer the company of the kafirun, knowing the harm they can cause, to the company of Muslims, we will risk losing Allah's guidance, security and protection. This does not imply total avoidance of Jews, Christians and pagans. It merely advises us to shorten the amount of time we spend with them to protect ourselves from compromising or weakening in our deen.:

You who have iman! do not take the Jews and Christians as your friends; they are the friends of one another. Any of you who takes them as friends is one of them. Allah does not guide wrongdoing people. (Surat al-Ma'idah 5: 51)

&

The muminun should not take kafirun as friends rather than muminun. Anyone who does that has nothing to do with Allah at all – unless it is because you are afraid of them. Allah advises you to be afraid of Him. Allah is the final destination. (Surat Al 'Imran 3: 28)

The Prophet (SAAS) advised all Muslims to keep good company with muminun who have taqwa, as they will encourage us to do right actions and refrain from doing wrong actions. They will constantly remind us of Allah (SWT) and steer us back onto the straight path towards the Garden:

You who have iman! have taqwa of Allah and be with the sadiqun (the truthful). (Surat at-Tawbah 9: 119)

&

Restrain yourself patiently with those who call on their

Lord morning and evening, desiring His face. Do not turn your eyes from them, desiring the attractions of this world. And do not obey someone whose heart We have made neglectful of Our remembrance and who follows his own whims and desires and whose life has transgressed all bounds. (Surat al-Kahf 18: 28)

The company we keep will not only determine our position in this life, but also our final position in the Hereafter. We should therefore, be selective in our choice of friends to ensure a better position in this life and the Next.

Spiritual Obligations Towards Fellow Sisters

A Compassionate Community

The Muslim community should be based upon sincere mutual love and respect, compassion, consideration and co-operation. We should all be concerned for the social, spiritual and emotional welfare of our fellow sisters-in-Islam and rely upon one another for comfort and support in times of need. Strong, reliable support networks should also be established in the community for women to access, such as mosques, Muslim women community organisations, support groups and telephone help lines etc. (For Muslim Women's Helpline in London ring 0181 908 6715)

> The Prophet (SAAS) said: "The relationship of a mumin to another mumin is like a building, one part of which supports others." (He intertwined his fingers). (Abu Musa (RA), Muslim Vol. IVA, p182, No. 2585. Also al-Bukhari. Vol. 8, p34, No. 55)
>
> &
>
> The likeness of the believers in their mutual affection, sympathy and compassion is like the body which when any of its members suffers from a complaint, the rest of the body rallies round with fever and sleeplessness. (an-Nu'man ibn Bashir (RA), al-Bukhari & Muslim. Also *Riyad as-Salihin*, Vol. I, p113, No. 224)

Every one of us should be a reliable and dependable member of the community. If a sister is in need, we should make every effort to make sure her needs are met. If a sister is troubled or feeling low in iman, we should remind her of Allah (SWT) and encourage her in the deen with spiritual comfort and support and with words of wisdom from the Qur'an and the Sunnah. If a sister is sick, we should make every effort to visit her and ensure she has all the necessary help and provisions, i.e. medicine, groceries, childcare and domestic assistance etc. If a Muslim woman is struggling financially, we should seek appropriate ways to help alleviate her burden, i.e. offer advice, or a loan or charitable donation, if we have the means. Assistance should be offered to fellow Muslim women whether they are young or old, single, married or divorced, with or without children or other dependants. Although they may have husbands or family and relatives living close by, it does not necessarily mean they are receiving support or coping well throughout their hardships. Appearances can be deceptive. Some Muslim women put on a brave face to hide their insecurities and weaknesses, while others may be too afraid, overwhelmed or embarrassed to ask for help. In some cases Muslim women just do not know how to ask for help. This is why we should always offer our help and support, even if it appears that it may not be needed. At least Allah (SWT) will reward us for having good intentions and for showing sympathy, compassion and concern for our Muslim brethren.

> **Hold fast to the rope of Allah all together, and do not separate. Remember Allah's blessing to you when you were enemies and He joined your hearts together so that you became brothers by His blessing. (Surat Al 'Imran 3: 103)**

If we help to ease the burden of a fellow sister-in-Islam, Allah (SWT) will ease our burdens when we are in need, both in this life and the Next and particularly on the Day of Rising.

> If anyone relieves his brother's anxiety in this world, Allah will remove one of his anxieties of the Day of Rising. If anyone makes it easy for an impoverished man, Allah will make it easy for him in this world and on the Day of Rising. If anyone conceals a Muslim's secrets, Allah will conceal his secrets in this world and on the Day of Rising. Allah will remain aiding a slave so long as the slave aids his brother.' (Abu Hurairah (RA), Abu Dawud, Vol. III, p1376, No. 4928. 'Abdullah ibn 'Umar (RA), Abu Dawud, Vol. III, p1363, No. 4875)

Encouraging One Another in Iman

> None of you has iman until he loves for his brother or for his neighbour what he loves for himself. (Anas ibn Malik (RA), Muslim, Vol. I, p37, No. 45. Anas (RA), al-Bukhari, Vol. I, p19, No. 12)

One characteristic of iman is wanting the same for our fellow sisters-in-Islam as we want for ourselves. If we ask Allah (SWT) to grant us a good position in the Garden, we should also ask Allah (SWT) to grant it to our fellow sisters. Allah (SWT) has specifically commanded us to help and encourage one another in iman and to enjoin the right and refrain from the wrong. If Muslim women are disobedient to Allah then we are duty-bound to correct them and guide them. Correction should be through verbal or physical instruction, i.e. through gentle speech or action, or at the very least, we should hate the wrong action in our hearts. However, the latter reflects the weakest iman. Instead of remaining silent and inactive we should change wrongdoing with our tongue or hand. When other Muslim women are present, it may be more diplomatic to keep quiet and correct her later when no one is around, to save her from any unnecessary public humiliation or embarrassment. However, if we do not correct her at all and remain silent every time she commits the wrong deed, it may give her the false impression that Islam condones the act, when in fact, it does not. If we know the correct way to behave, we should always guide other Muslim women to do the same. If we fail to guide her, Allah (SWT) may judge us for withholding Islamic knowledge. He (SWT) may also judge us for failing to help or advise a fellow sister when she needs it most. When we guide other sisters to do right actions, we will be given the same reward as the sister, who does the good deed, even if we do not do it ourselves.

Let there be a community among you who call to the good, and enjoin the right, and forbid the wrong. They are the ones who have success. (Surah Al 'Imran 3: 104)

&

Whoever of you sees something objectionable then let him change it with his hand, and if he is not able then with his tongue, and if he is not able then with his heart, and that is the weakest iman (Abu Sa'id al-Khudri (RA), Muslim, Vol. IA, p39, No. 49)

&

If anyone guides someone to a good deed, he will receive a reward like the reward of the one who does it. (Abu Mas'ud (RA), Abu Dawud, Vol. III, p1420, No. 5110)

Although we should guide Muslim women towards good Islamic practice, Allah (SWT) may punish us if we offer them incorrect advice, depending on our intention. We should never advise others according to how we think or feel, or pass our own fatwas (Islamic rulings) since almost none of us have the comprehensive knowledge in fiqh (Islamic jurisprudence) which would qualify us to do that. Instead we should offer advice with authentic Islamic knowledge and provide reliable evidence from the Qur'an and Sunnah or from reputable sheikhs and scholars.

> If anyone summons others to follow right guidance, his reward will be equivalent to those of the people who follow him without their reward being decreased in any way. And if anyone invites others to follow error, his wrongdoing will be equivalent to those who follow him without their wrongdoing being decreased in any way. (Abu Hurairah (RA), Abu Dawud, Vol. III, p1037, No. 3649. Muslim. Riyad as-Salihin,Vol. I, p91, No. 174)

> &

> If anyone interprets the book of Allah (the Qur'an) in the light of his opinion, even if he is right, he has erred. (Jundub (RA), Abu Dawud Vol. III, p1036, No. 3644.)

The last hadith means it is a serious wrong action to interpret the Qur'an without due knowledge and competence, even if the person is correct in their interpretation.

Praying with Sisters in Congregation

When Muslim women gather for a meeting and it approaches time for prayer, Imam Shafi'i felt that they should all pray together in congregation and in straight rows. He based this on a hadith Abu Hurairah (RA) (in al-Bukhari, Vol. 1, p388, No. 689). However, this was not the view of the other imams. The shoulders of each Muslim woman should also be touching those of the Muslim woman next to her. This will bring them closer together and prevent shaytan creating hostility in between the gaps. In Islam congregational prayer is twenty-seven times superior to the prayer said alone (as is Ibn 'Umar (RA) in a hadith agreed upon by al-Bukhari and Muslim. Riyad as-Salihin, Vol. II, p53, No. 1064):

> You must align your rows (in prayer), otherwise Allah will create differences among you (i.e. it will create enmity among you). (Abu 'Abdullah an-Nu'man ibn Bashir (RA). Agreed Upon. Riyad as-Salihin. Vol. I, p83, No. 160)

&

The Messenger of Allah (SAAS) paid attention to the people and said three times: "Straighten your rows in prayer; by Allah, you must straighten your rows, or Allah will certainly put your faces in contrary directions." I then saw that every person stood in prayer keeping his shoulder close to that of the other, and his knee close to that of the other, and his ankle close to that of the other. (an-Nu'man ibn Bashir (RA), Abu Dawud, Vol. I, p173, No. 662)

&

Set the rows in order, stand shoulder to shoulder, close the gaps, be pliant in the hands of your brethren, and do not leave openings for shaytan. If anyone joins up a row, Allah will join him up, but if anyone breaks a row, Allah will cut him off. ('Abdullah ibn 'Umar (RA), Abu Dawud, Vol. I, p173, No. 666)

In addition to the benefits already mentioned, congregational prayer also encourages us to improve the performance and practice of our prayer. For example, we are more likely to offer prayer close to its stated fixed time and offer more Sunnah prayers. It will also strengthen our guard against shaytan, who will try to distract the 'lone' Muslimah from her prayers:

If three men in a locality or in a desert make no arrangement for prayer in *jama'ah* (congregation), shaytan will overcome them. So observe prayer in congregation, for the wolf only eats solitary straggling sheep. (Abu'd-Darda (RA), Abu Dawud, *Riyad as-Salihin*, Vol. II, p55, No. 1070)

Another common distraction during the prayer is Muslim women walking in front of us before we have finished praying. This is something that is forbidden and should be actively discouraged but not with violence or verbal abuse. Children should be taught the adab of congregational prayer at a very early age, as they often like to run and play in front of Muslim women during salat. The following hadiths highlight the seriousness of passing in front of a Muslim when praying:

When any of you pray, he should not allow anyone to pass before him, and if he refuses, he should then be forcibly resisted, for there is a shaytan with him. ('Abdullah ibn 'Umar (RA),

Muslim, Vol. IB, p296, No. 506)

&

If anyone who passes in front of a man praying knew the responsibility he incurs, he would stand still for forty rather than pass in front of him. Abu Nadr said: "I do not know whether he said forty days or years." (Abu Juhaim al-Ansari (RA), Muslim, Vol. IB, p296, No. 507)

Remembering Sisters in Your Supplications

In Islam there is nothing more powerful than du'a (supplication), especially when the same du'a is invoked by many people at the same time. The Prophet (SAAS) said that the supplication that gains the quickest response is the one made by a Muslim for a fellow Muslim ('Abdullah ibn 'Amr ibn al-'As (RA), Abu Dawud, Vol. I, p398, No. 1530). He (SAAS) also said that if we supplicate Allah (SWT) for a fellow Muslim, the angels would supplicate for us.

When a Muslim supplicates for his absent brother, the angels say: "Ameen and may you receive the same too." (Abu'd-Darda (RA), Muslim, Vol. IVB, p250, No. 2732. Abu Dawud, Vol. I, Ch. 515, No.1529)

&

'Umar ibn al-Khattab (RA) said, "I sought permission of the Prophet (SAAS) to perform 'umrah. He gave me permission and said: 'My younger brother, do not forget me in your supplication.'" He (Umar) said: "He said a word that pleased me so much that I would not have been pleased if I were given the whole world." (Abu Dawud & at-Tirmidhi. *Riyad as-Salihin*, Vol. I, p164, No. 373)

Although it is permissible to supplicate for a person, scholars differ in their opinion as to whether it is permissible, using the word *salli*, to invoke blessings on a person other than the Prophet (SAAS). According to some, it is permissible unconditionally, while another view states it is only permissible for the Prophet (SAAS) and not for others. A third view states that one can invoke blessings using the word *salli* upon others along with the Prophet (SAAS) but not separately, while a fourth view states it is not permissible at all (Commentary taken from Abu Dawud, Vol. I, p398, Footnote 859).

Attitude and Behaviour Toward Fellow Sisters

Good character and behaviour hold the Muslim community together. Without good manners and social courtesy, disharmony and disunity would inevitably result. Muslims are advised to emulate the exemplary character of the Prophet (saas) and his companions, and mirror the best behaviour to one another. Muslims are ambassadors for Islam and should set high standards in their own character and conduct as examples for others to follow.

> The best among you are those who have the best manners and character. (Masruq (RA), al-Bukhari, Vol. 8, p35, No. 56b. Also Abu Hurairah (RA), Abu Dawud, Vol. III, p1312, No. 4665)

Although Islamic courtesy is required of every Muslim, it is appalling to see how ill-mannered and rude some Muslim women can be. For example: some may forget to acknowledge or thank one another for their small acts of kindness. The Prophet (SAAS) warned that if we are ungrateful to others we are actually being ungrateful to Allah (SWT)! (Abu Hurairah (RA), Abu Dawud Vol. III, p1346, No. 4793. Also in Ahmad and at-Tirmidhi) Unfortunately, poor manners are often ignored, overlooked or excused, and although it is good to excuse the failings of a fellow Muslim, we should in fact, remind one another to adopt good manners. This will now be discussed in more detail with supporting evidence from the Qur'an and the Sunnah.

Good Manners

> **The slaves of the All-Merciful are those who walk lightly on the earth and, who, when the ignorant speak to them, say, 'Peace'. (Surat al-Furqan 25: 63)**

&

The Prophet (SAAS) said: "If gentleness is found in anything, it beautifies it and if it is withdrawn from anything it damages it and makes it defective." (al-Miqdam ibn Shuraih (RA), Abu

Dawud, Vol. III, p1345, No. 4790. Also A'ishah (RA), Muslim, Vol. IVA, p185, No. 2594) He (SAAS) also said: "He who is deprived of gentleness is deprived of good." (Jarir (RA), Abu Dawud, Vol. III, p1345, No. 4791)

Good manners are essential in a Muslim's character. They help to maintain harmonious relations and are vital for pacifying tense or difficult situations and thus prevent hostility and bad feeling. Good manners require polite, modest speech, discretion and a certain amount of tact and diplomacy. They also require us to exercise patience, be kind and humble in our conduct and have consideration for others. Good manners are important when giving effective da'wah to argumentative non-Muslims or encouraging weak sisters to practice. If our words are too harsh or insensitive, they will either fall upon deaf ears or antagonise the listener. When we talk about Islam, it is important to consider the attitude and mentality of our audience. There is no point in talking about issues that require high levels of iman when the audience has not even grasped the most fundamental beliefs in Islam. We should also refrain from frightening people with constant reminders of punishment in the Fire. Instead, we should remind them of Allah's mercy and blessings, and His rewards for doing good deeds. We should talk about Islam with wisdom and in an easy manner so other Muslim women will feel encouraged to practise. (Commentary taken from Abu Dawud Vol. III, p1350, Footnote 4204)

> **Call to the way of your Lord with wisdom and fair admonition, and argue with them in the kindest way. Your Lord knows best who is misguided from His way. And He knows best who are guided. (Surat an-Nahl 16: 125)**
>
> &
>
> Gladden people and do not scare them; make things easy and do not make them difficult. (Abu Musa (RA), Abu Dawud, Vol. III, p1050, No. 4817)

Good manners reflect iman and character. They will also protect us from punishment in the Fire and ensure a better position in the Garden (insha'Allah). The rewards for good manners are as follows:

> The heaviest thing which will be placed in the balance of a slave who is mumin on the Day of Judgement will be that [placed in the balance of one] who has good manners.' (Abu ad-Darda

(RA), at-Tirmidhi. Also *Riyad as-Salihin*, Vol. I, p253, No. 626)

&

A mumin will attain the rank of one who prays during the night and fasts during the day by his good character. (A'ishah (RA), Abu Dawud. Also *Riyad as-Salihin*, Vol. I, p254, No. 629. Also *Muwatta al-Imam Malik*, p377, No. 1612)

&

I guarantee a house in the surroundings of the Garden for a man who avoids quarrelling even if he is in the right, a house in the middle of the Garden for a man who avoids lying even if he is joking, and a house in the upper part of Garden for a man who makes his character good. (Abu Umamah (RA), Abu Dawud, Vol. III, p1344, No. 4782)

Love for Fellow Sisters

The Prophet (SAAS) said that love for a fellow Muslim is an important aspect of iman. It helps to strengthen ties in the Muslim ummah (community) and prevent unnecessary division. To love a fellow sister for Allah's sake also helps to perfect our own iman.

> You will not enter the Garden until you affirm your iman (in all those things that are articles of iman) and you will not have iman until you love one another. Should I not direct you a thing which, if you do, will foster love amongst you? (i.e) Spread the [practice of salutation to one another by saying] as-salaamu [alaikum]. (Abu Hurairah (RA), Muslim, Vol. I, p44, No. 54)

&

> If anyone loves for Allah's sake, hates for Allah's sake, gives for Allah's sake and withholds for Allah's sake, he will have perfected iman.' (Abu Umamah (RA), Abu Dawud, Vol. III, p1312, No. 3664)

If Allah (SW) commands us to love one another for His sake, our likes or dislikes should never be merely for our own sake. Similarly we should not display love and affection for any selfish motive or worldly material gain, i.e. for what another Muslim woman can offer us in return. We should love a fellow Muslim woman for her strength of iman and good character and her ability to enjoin what Allah (SW) commands and refrain from what He has prohibited. If a Muslim woman fails to obey Allah (SWT), she will lose the love of Allah (SWT) and the love of her fellow sisters-in-Islam.

If we love a fellow sister we should always let her know, as this causes mutual love to grow and sincere friendship to develop.

> When a man loves his brother, he should tell him that he loves him. (al-Miqdam ibn Ma'dikarib (RA), Abu Dawud, Vol. III, p1419, No. 5105)

> &

> A man was with the Prophet (SAAS) and another man passed by and [the first man] said: "Messenger of Allah! I love this man." The Prophet (SAAS) then asked: "Have you told him?" He replied "No." He said: "Tell him." He went to him and said: "I love you for Allah's sake." He replied: "May He for whose sake you love me love you." (Anas ibn Malik (RA), Abu Dawud, Vol. III, p1419, No. 5106)

Allah (SWT) loves those who love each other for His sake. He will also shelter them in His shadow and elevate them upon pillars of light on the Day of Judgement, as the following hadiths re-iterate:

> There are three qualities for which anyone who is characterised by them will relish the sweetness of faith: he whom Allah and His Messenger are dearer to him than any other thing: who loves a man for Allah's sake alone; and who hates to return to kufr after Allah has rescued him from it as he hates being cast into Fire. (Anas ibn Malik (RA), al-Bukhari, Vol. p42, No.67. Muslim, Vol. I, p36)

> &

> Allah will say on the Day of Rising: Where are those who love each other for My sake? Today I shall shelter them in My shade where there is no other shade than My shade.' (Abu Hurairah (RA), Muslim, Vol. IV, p175, No. 2566)

> &

> Allah (SWT) says: "Those who have mutual love for the sake of Allah, without any mutual kinship or giving property to each other, there will be light on their faces, and they will be sitting

on pillars of light and will be envied by the prophets and martyrs. ('Umar ibn al-Khattab (RA), Abu Dawud, Vol. II, p1001, No. 3520)

&

A man visited his brother in another town and Allah deputed an angel to wait for him on his way and when he came to him he said: "Where do you intend to go?" He said: " I intend to go to my brother in this town," he said: "Have you done any favour to him (the repayment of which you intend to get)?" He said: "No, except that I love him for the sake of Allah, the Exalted and Glorious." There upon he said: "I am a messenger to you from Allah (to inform you) that Allah loves you as you love him (for His sake)." (Abu Hurairah (RA), Muslim, Vol. IV, p175, No. 2567)

Allah (SWT) loves those who love one another for His sake and will instruct all of His creation in the heavens and the earth to love them too, as it states in the following hadith:

> If Allah loves a person, He calls Jibril saying "Allah loves so and so; Jibril love him." Jibril will love him and then Jibril will make an announcement among the residents of the heaven, "Allah loves so and so, therefore you should love him also." So, all the residents of the heavens would love him and then he is granted the pleasure of the people of the earth, i.e. the people of taqwa and the right-acting people of the world know him to be endeared and love him too. When Allah is angry with a slave, Malik said, "I consider that he says the like of that about His anger." (Abu Hurairah (RA), al-Bukhari Vol 8, p41, No. 66. Also *Muwatta al-Imam Malik,* p403, No. 1716)

The Rights of a Sister over Another Sister

A fundamental principle of sisterhood requires all Muslim women have the same basic understanding of Islam. This understanding should be based solely on the Qur'an and Sunnah of Prophet Muhammad (saas). The Muslim woman must then be aware of her obligations as a Muslim, firstly towards Allah (swt), then the Prophet (saas), then her family and peers in the community. She must then do her best to fulfil her expected roles, duties and obligations. As Muslims we have God-given rights over one another. Six of these rights are outlined in the following hadith:

> A Muslim has six rights over another Muslim: when you meet him, offer him greetings; when he invites you [to a wedding feast] accept it; when he seeks counsel give him; and when he sneezes and says al-hamdulillah (Praise is to Allah), you say yarhamuka'llah (may Allah show mercy to you) and when he is ill visit him; and when he dies follow his bier. (Abu Hurairah (RA), Muslim, Vol. III, p437, No. 2162R4)

Although it is not totally prohibited, women are not advised to attend funeral processions. This is because women usually find it more difficult to control their emotions than men and may draw unnecessary attention to themselves. However, sisters can join the *janazah* prayer in the mosque, and supplicate on behalf of the deceased. Supplication is important, as Allah (swt) will accept the intercession of forty Muslims (or more), who ask forgiveness on behalf of the deceased Muslim, as the following hadiths affirm:

> Umm 'Atiyyah (RA) said: We were forbidden to accompany funeral processions [but not strictly]. (al-Bukhari, Vol. 2, p206, No. 368. Also Muslim, Vol. IIA, p53, Nos. 938 & 938R1)

&

> If any Muslim dies and forty men who associate nothing with

Allah stand over his prayer (offer prayer over him), Allah will accept them as intercessors for him. ('Abdullah ibn 'Abbas (RA), Muslim, Vol. IIA, p60, No. 948)

&

If a company of Muslims numbering one hundred pray over a dead person, all of them interceding for him, their intercession will be accepted. (A'ishah (RA), Muslim, Vol. IIA, p59, No. 947)

There is no contradiction between the first and second hadith. Here we have been told that forty God-fearing men can successfully intercede for the dead. If the number increases the intercession will inevitably become more effective. (Commentary taken from Muslim, Vol. II, p60, Footnote 3)

Worship Allah and do not associate anything with Him. Be good to your parents and relatives and to orphans and the very poor, and to neighbours who are related to you and neighbours who are not related to you, and to companions and travellers and your slaves. Allah does not love anyone vain or boastful. (Surat an-Nisa 4: 36)

In Islam we also have certain obligations towards and rights over our neighbours. This not only applies to Muslim neighbours but also to those who are non-Muslim. We should maintain good relations with them and keep them safe from our harm and mischief. If we are impolite, inconsiderate or abusive, Allah (SWT) may not allow us to enter the Garden on the Day of Judgement. (Abu Hurairah (RA), Muslim. Also *Riyadh as-Salihin*, (Arabic – English version), Vol. 1, p192, No. 305) Instead we should be considerate of their feelings and show sincere concern for their welfare and wellbeing. We should also try to give them the best of what we have, e.g. food, money or possessions, and ensure that their needs are sufficiently met.

A'ishah (RA) asked the Prophet (SAAS): "I have two neighbours, to whom shall I send a present?" He said: "To the one whose door is nearer to yours." (Al-Bukhari. Also *Riyadh as-Salihin*, (Arabic – English version), Vol. 1, p194, No. 310)

&

The Prophet (SAAS) said: "When you prepare soup put a little more water in it and see if your neighbour needs some." (Abu

Dharr (RA), Muslim. Also *Riyadh as-Salihin*, (Arabic – English version), Vol. 1, p192, No. 304)

&

The Prophet (SAAS) said, "Jibril kept instructing me about obligations towards the neighbour, so much so, I imagined that he might be included as one of the heirs with rights to inheritance!" (A'ishah (RA), al-Bukhari & Muslim. Also *Riyadh as-Salihin,* (Arabic – English version), Vol. 1, p192, No. 303)

Meeting and Greeting Sisters

It is obligatory for Muslims to greet (with salaam) one another, as it helps to spread love and compassion between them. (al-Bara ibn 'Azib (RA), al-Bukhari, Vol. 8, p166, No. 253. Also Muslim) Greeting (salaam) should also be initiated before talking or striking up a conversation. (Jabir (RA), at-Tirmidhi) This is something we should remember, not only in our personal meetings, but also in our telephone conversations and written correspondence. The Muslim who greets with salaam first is the one who is best in conduct. She may also be the one who is nearest to Allah (SWT). (Umamah &Abu Umamah (RA), Abu Dawud, Vol. III, p1435, No. 5178. Also Ahmad, at-Tirmidhi and Riyad as-Salihin, Vol. I, p324, No. 858) Allah (SWT) instructs us to respond to a greeting with one that is either better than or equal to the greeting we receive:

> **When you are greeted with a greeting, return the greeting or improve on it. Allah takes account of everything. (Surat an-Nisa 4: 86)**

The Islamic greeting of salaam is as follows:

As-salaamu 'alaikum (Peace be upon you)

(The reward for this salaam is worth ten good deeds),

or

As-salamu 'alaikum wa-ratmatu'llah (Peace and the mercy of Allah be upon you)

(The reward for this salaam is worth twenty good deeds),

or

As-salaamu 'alaikum wa ramatullahi wa barakatuh (Peace and the mercy of Allah and His blessings be upon you)

(The reward for this salaam is worth thirty good deeds), ('Imran ibn Husayn (RA), Abu Dawud, Vol. III, p1434, No. 5176. Also At-Tirmidhi and in Riyad as-Salihin, Vol. I, p323, No 851)

These rewards are based upon the principle that a good deed will receive a ten-fold reward. The rewards naturally increase according to the words added to the salutation. (Commentary taken from Abu Dawud, Vol. III, p1434, Footnote 4484)

The reply is as follows:

Wa 'alaikum as-salaam (and upon you be peace)

Or

Wa 'alaikum as-salaam wa rahmatullah (and upon you be peace and Allah's mercy)

Returning the greeting of other Muslims is obligatory in Islam. If we see a Muslim woman in the street, supermarket, mosque, at a talk or special function, we should always give her the greeting of salaam, whether we know her or not.

Good deeds in Islam are to feed the poor and greet those whom you know and those whom you don't know. ('Abdullah ibn 'Amr (RA), al-Bukhari, Vol. 1, p28, No. 27)

Sadly, we may not always receive a polite or favourable response. Instead, we may be looked down upon, scowled at or blatantly ignored. These ill-mannered responses may either be due to ignorance, arrogance or shyness on part of the sister who does not return the greeting. However, if she knew the rewards for initiating the Islamic greeting or returning it, she would rush to do it. It is possible that she does not know the rewards for offering salaams. In which case, it is our duty to remind her, gently and tactfully. We are also recommended to smile when we greet one another, as it is a good deed highly rewarded by Allah (SWT).

The Prophet (SAAS) was asked which Islamic traits are the best, and he replied: "...to greet those whom you know and those whom you do not know." ('Abdullah ibn 'Amr (RA), al-Bukhari, Vol. 8, p167, No. 253)

&

Every good deed of a Muslim is sadaqah, and meeting your

Muslim brother with a smiling face is one of the good deeds. (Jabir (RA), Abu Dawud and at-Tirmidhi)

&

Don't consider any of the good things insignificant even if it is that you meet your brother with a cheerful countenance. (Abu Dharr (RA), Muslim, Vol. IVA, p201, No. 2626)

The greeting (*salaam*) may be repeated if an object such as a tree, a wall or a person intervenes between two sisters and they meet again, or when one of them departs for a brief period and then returns, i.e. to retrieve something while on the phone:

When one of you meets a brother, he should salute him. Then if a tree, or a wall, or a stone intervenes between them and then he meets him again, he should salute him. (Abu Hurairah (RA), Abu Dawud, Vol. III, p1435, No. 5181)

The adab (courtesy) of the salaam depends upon the social setting, and the position or status of the individuals involved. These are as follows:

A small number of persons should greet a large number of persons. (Abu Hurairah (RA), al-Bukhari, Vol. 8, p165, No. 250)

When a Muslim woman or a small group of Muslim women attend a large social gathering, they should always greet the larger group with salaam first, and do the same when they depart, as the first act of greeting earns the same rewards as the last. (Abu Hurairah (RA), Abu Dawud, Vol. III, p1437, No. 5189. Also at-Tirmidhi)

The young should greet the old,... (Abu Hurairah (RA), al-Bukhari, Vol. 8, p165, No. 250)

&

...the walking should greet the sitting ... (Abu Hurairah (RA), al-Bukhari, Vol. 8, p165, No. 252. Also Muslim,Vol. IIIB, p436)

&

The mounted should first greet the walking ... (Abu Hurairah (RA), Muslim, Vol. III, p436, No. 2160)

We can also send salaams to an absent sister via another sister. When the absent Muslim woman receives the salaam, she should respond in a similar way as did A'ishah (RA) when Jibril (AS) sent his salaams to her via the Prophet (SAAS). Her response was as follows:

> *Wa 'alaihi's-salaam wa ratmatu'llah* (and upon him peace and Allah's mercy) (A'ishah (RA), al-Bukhari, Vol. 8, p178, No. 270. A similar hadith was Ghalib (RA), Abu Dawud, Vol. III, p1443, No. 5212)

or as in another case:

> *Wa 'alaiha's-salaam wa ratmatu'llah* (and on her peace and Allah's mercy)

N.B. (*'alaihi* is male, *'alaiha* is female;)

We are also advised to shake hands with one another when we greet, as this helps to remove enmity or any potential dislike. Allah (SWT) will also expiate our wrong actions before we separate. This was a noted custom of the Prophet (SAAS) and his companions, and can either be performed using one hand or both hands. Another noted custom was to embrace a fellow Muslim by placing one's arms around their neck (*al-Mu'anaqah*). (Ibn Mas'ud and by Qatadah (RA), al-Bukhari, Vol. 8, p186, No. 278-80)

> Shake hands one with the other, the spite of the heart will vanish. Send presents one to the other, and you will be friends, enmity will disappear. ('Ata al-Khurasani (RA), *Muwatta al-Imam Malik,* p379, No. 1622)

&

> Two Muslims will not meet and shake hands without having their wrong actions forgiven before they separate. (al-Bara (RA), Abu Dawud, Vol. III, p1438, No. 5193. In another narration al-Bara says: "If two Muslims meet, shake hands, praise Allah and ask Him for forgiveness, they will be forgiven.")

Celebrations and Conveying Glad Tidings

One of the six rights a Muslim has over another Muslim is that he accept an invitation to a wedding feast, which is obligatory, and it is even highly recommended to accept a dinner invitation, a celebration for the birth of a baby (*'aqiqah*) etc. As well as accepting social invitations, it is also important for Muslims to wish one another well. Once a social invitation has been accepted, every effort should be made to keep to the agreed appointment. If there is a need to change, postpone or cancel the appointment, it should be for a valid reason, and plenty of warning should be given beforehand. The sister does not necessarily need to know the reason in great detail, but it is only polite to provide her with reasonable justification for the cancellation. Ultimately, Allah (SWT) will judge us according to our intentions.

> The Messenger of Allah (SAAS) said, "The deen is sincerity." We said, "For whom?" He said, "For Allah, His Book, His Messenger, the leaders of the Muslims and their generality." (Tamim ad-Dari (RA), Muslim, Vol. IA, p45, No. 55)

There are three opinions concerning the acceptance of a wedding invitation. The first states that it is desirable and obligatory for all those invited to attend, unless one has a valid excuse. The second opinion states that it is a collective obligation (*fard kifayah*), i.e. some people must attend it and the third opinion states it is commendable to attend it. According to some Shafi' scholars, it is obligatory to accept all invitations, whether it is a marriage invitation or otherwise, while Malik and most of the scholars hold that it is commendable to attend celebrations other than marriage celebrations. ('Awn al-Ma'bud, III, 394. Commentary taken from Abu Dawud, Vol. III, p1056, Footnote 3175) According to al-Baghawi it is permissible to decline the invitation if there is a good excuse (such as fear that there will be alcohol present) or the location of the celebration is difficult to reach. (*Fiqh as-Sunnah*, Sayyid Sabiq, Vol. III, p108) It is unanimously agreed, however, that no one should attend a feast without an invitation, as it may cause bad feeling and hostility to the host.

> When one of you is invited for a wedding feast, he must attend it. ('Abdullah ibn 'Umar (RA), Abu Dawud, Vol. III, p1056, No. 3727)

&

> Those who do not accept the invitation have disobeyed Allah and His Messenger. (Abu Hurairah (RA), *Fiqh as-Sunnah*, Sayyid Sabiq, p106, No. 4.2)

According to Imam at-Tirmidhi, it is not permissible to accept the invitation of those whose income is haram (illegitimate). However, there is scope for accepting the invitation if their earnings consist of both halal and haram (legitimate and illegitimate) incomes. (at-Tirmidhi, Ch. XXXI, p136) However, in situations such as these, it may not be easy to ascertain the lawfulness of a Muslim's income. In addition we should avoid suspicion and refrain from listening to gossip or hearsay concerning such matters. Instead we should act upon reliable and credible evidence and information sources. False allegations and slander are serious offences in Islam and worthy of punishment in the Fire. It is then perhaps better in dubious situations to accept the invitation and leave Allah (SWT) to judge the financial circumstances of one's host. And Allah knows best.

When a Muslim marries, it is obligatory to inform the community, and invite them to celebrate the marriage and to offer congratulations and gifts (their offering gifts is recommended but not compulsory). It is also important to inform the community about a marriage as it may prevent unnecessary rumour and gossip. To illustrate this point, if a Muslim woman is seen with her new husband in public, and the marriage has not been broadcast to the community, she could be accused of committing *zina* (adultery). Mistakes such as these can easily be avoided by making the marriage public at the time of the contract or soon after with a *walimah*.

> The walimah (wedding banquet) is obligatory. And 'Abd ar-Rahman ibn 'Auf said: "The Prophet (SAAS) said to me: 'Give a wedding banquet, even with one sheep.'" ('Abd ar-Rahman ibn 'Auf (RA), al-Bukhari, Vol. 7, p70)

An 'aqiqah is a form of sadaqah (charity), whereby sheep are sacrificed on the seventh day following the birth of a child. One sheep is sacrificed for the birth of a girl, while the majority of scholars hold that two sheep are sacrificed for the birth of a boy. The child's head is shaved, and the weight of the hair in silver is given as sadaqah to the poor. This is offered as a token of gratitude to Allah (SWT) for blessing them with a child. The child should also be given a name by the seventh day while some hold that boys should be circumcised within this time, although Imam Malik strongly disapproved of it at that age. Although it is not obligatory for the parents to bring the community together for a feast, (Commentary taken from Abu Dawud, Vol. II, p797, Footnote 2218) it is a nice gesture and an ideal opportunity to share the blessings and welcome a new member to the Muslim community.

> A boy is in pledge for his *'aqiqah*; sacrifice is made for him on the seventh day, his head is shaved and he is given a name. (Samura ibn Jundub (RA), Ahmad and also at-Tirmidhi)

Visiting Sisters

When visiting a sister, good adab (courtesy) dictates that you should contact her beforehand to arrange a mutually appropriate time to arrive. However, on some occasions an impromptu visit may not allow sufficient prior warning. If we visit a fellow sister at her house and there is no response, it is recommended to knock no more than three times. (Abu Sa'id al-Khudri (RA), al-Bukhari, Vol. 8, p173, No. 262. Also Abu Dawud, Vol. III, p1429, No. 5161. Abu Musa al-Ash'ari (RA), *Muwatta al-Imam Malik,* p407, No. 1737) If after the third attempt there is still no answer we should leave, as this indicates that it is either an unsuitable time to visit or the sister is not at home. We should never enter another person's house without being invited or seeking permission to enter first. The Muslim woman is then entitled to allow entry or refuse it.

> **You who have iman! do not enter houses other than your own until you have asked permission and greeted their inhabitants. That is better for you, so that hopefully you will pay heed. And if you find no one at home do not go in until permission has been granted you. And if you are told to go away then go away. That is purer for you. Allah knows what you do. (Surat an-Nur 24: 27-28)**

It is wrong to enter and look around someone's house without their permission, as it is an invasion of their privacy and we may hear or see something we should not, e.g. a person in a state of undress, or an untidy house and so on.

> **...And do not spy... (Surat al-Hujurat 49: 12)**

&

If anyone peeps into the house of a person without their permission and he knocks out his eye, no responsibility is incurred for his eye. (Abu Hurairah (RA), Abu Dawud, Vol. III, p1428, No. 5153)

&

...and he who enters without invitation enters as a thief and goes out as a raider. ('Abdullah ibn 'Umar (RA), Abu Dawud, Vol. III, p1056, No. 3732)

Before entering the house, we should exchange greetings (salaams) and ask permission to enter, unless we have already been invited in. We should also ask the Muslim woman if there are men in the house, i.e. her husband, father or brother. If men are present one should observe the Islamic adab (courtesy) of gender segregation.

> **And when you enter houses greet one another with a greeting from Allah, blessed and good. (Surat an-Nur 24: 59)** (i.e. say *as-salamu 'alaikum* – peace be upon you).

> &

> A man of Banu 'Amir asked permission to enter the house of the Prophet (SAAS) saying: "May I enter?" The Prophet (SAAS) said to his servant: 'Go out to this man and teach him how to ask permission to enter the house, and say to him; "Say: peace be upon you. May I enter?" The man heard it and said: "Peace be upon you! May I enter?" The Prophet (SAAS) permitted him and he entered. (Rib'i ibn Hirash (RA), Abu Dawud, Vol. III, p1429, No. 5158. A similar hadith is narrated by Kilda ibn al-Hanbal (RA), at-Tirmidhi. Also *Riyad as-Salihin*, Vol. I, p328, No. 873)

It is also recommended to observe and respect the customs of the house, i.e. to remove one's shoes by the front door; not to enter other rooms in the house without being invited; not to remove hijab without first ensuring the absence of men and so on.

Generosity

In Islam, it is recommended to show utmost kindness and generosity towards others. There are also many rewards for giving people the best of what we have, especially if it is something we cherish or appreciate most:

> A generous person is close to Allah, close to the Garden, close to people and far away from the Fire. A miser is far from Allah, far from the Garden, far from people and close to the Fire. An ordinary, generous person is dearer to Allah than a religious miser. (Abu Hurairah (RA), at-Tirmidhi)

> &

> Spend, do not hold back and do not keep what is left over, otherwise Allah will also hold back from you. (Asma bint Abi Bakr (RA), al-Bukhari and Muslim)

The poor are also advised to give generously, even if they can only spare half a date. Alternatively, a good, friendly word can be spoken and offered as sadaqah, and words require no more than a little effort. Making du'a (supplication) for a fellow Muslim is also a priceless gift for which money or material wealth can never substitute.

> Guard yourselves against the Fire of Hell, even if it be only with half a date given in sadaqah; and that whoever cannot afford even that should at least utter a good word. ('Adi ibn Hatim (RA), Agreed upon. Riyad as-Salihin, Vol. I, p276, No.693)

&

> A good, pleasant, friendly word is a sadaqah. (Abu Hurairah (RA), al-Bukhari, Vol. 8, Ch.34, p32)

Giving and Receiving Gifts

In Islam it is recommended to exchange gifts with one another as it helps to increase mutual love and affection and remove any potential ill feeling. All gifts should be offered with good intentions and not for any personal or selfish gain, i.e. as a bribe, or to impress or influence people.

> Exchange gifts with one another, for gifts remove ill will from people's hearts. (Ai'shah (RA), at-Tirmidhi)

&

> Allah's messenger (SAAS) used to accept gifts and used to give something in return. (A'ishah (RA), al-Bukhari, Vol. 3, p458, No. 758)

All gifts whether large or small if accepted should be with sincere appreciation and gratitude. We should always remember the famous adage; 'it is the thought that counts...' rather than the type, size or price tag attached to it. A gift should not be returned to the one who offered it, as it may offend them. Declining a gift also denies the sister her chance of gaining rewards from Allah (SWT). Similarly we should never take back a gift once we have given it. The Prophet (SAAS) likened this abhorrent and detestable act to a dog that swallows its own vomit. (Ibn Abbas (RA), al-Bukhari, Vol. 3, p461, No. 762) In another narration he states that someone who takes back his gift is like a dog that vomits and returns to eat it. (Riyad as-Salihin, Vol. II, p220)

> Muslim women! None of you should look down upon a gift sent by her she-neighbour even if it were the trotters of the sheep (its feet). (Abu Hurairah (RA), al-Bukhari, Vol. 3, p447, No. 740)

> &

> For someone who gives a she-camel as a gift there is the reward (of the gift) both morning and evening, a reward for drinking milk in the morning and a reward for drinking milk in the evening. (Abu Hurairah (RA), Muslim, Vol. IIIA, p102, No. 1020)

A gift that offers benefit or aid to a fellow Muslim is the one that receives the greatest reward. For example, Islamic knowledge and books provide great benefit to sisters and also earn recurring reward every time the knowledge is remembered and put into practice. Conveying knowledge will also continue to earn rewards for us even after our death. (Abu Hurairah (RA), *Riyad as-Salihin*, Vol. II, p136, No. 1383)

Adab (courtesy) in Social Gatherings

If a group of sisters are sitting together in a social gathering, it is discourteous to separate them by coming between them, unless they give permission for you to do so. ('Amr ibn Shu'aib (RA), Abu Dawud Vol. III, p1352, No. 4826. Also at-Tirmidhi. Riyad as-Salihin, Vol. I, p317, No. 829) Similarly, it is discourteous to force a Muslim woman to give up her seat. Instead she has to be willing to give it up voluntarily without coercion. However, by the same token it is the duty of all Muslim women in an assembly to make room for other sisters to sit down.

> A man should not make another man get up from his seat in a gathering in order to sit there. (Ibn 'Umar (RA), al-Bukhari, Vol. 8, p191, No. 286)

> &

> It is the duty of a Muslim to move aside for him and let him join the gathering. (Wathilah ibn al-Khattab (RA), al-Bayhaqi)

> &

> **You who have iman! when you are told: 'Make room in the gathering,' then make room ... (Surat al-Mujadilah 58: 11)**

If a Muslim woman leaves her seat for a brief period, but wishes to return to it later on, the seat should be offered back to her, as the following hadith states:

> When someone gets up from his seat and returns to it, he is more entitled to it. (Abu Hurairah (RA), Muslim. Also *Riyad as-Salihin*, Vol. I, p316, No. 826. Also Abu Dawud, Vol. III, p1354, No. 4835)

Entertaining Sisters and Guests

The general principle for entertaining guests, according to the Islamic Shar'iah is as follows:

> 1. The guest is to be entertained for three days. On the first day, the host should take the trouble to show them utmost kindness and courtesy.
>
> 2. On the second and third days, the host should offer their guest what they have at hand, not exceeding the usual custom; then
>
> 3. The host should give their guest enough provisions to journey for a day and a night, and whatever is given after that, shall be given as sadaqah and an act of favour. (Commentary No. 2 from Muslim, Vol III, p159)
>
> He who believes in Allah and the Hereafter should show respect to the guest even with the utmost kindness and courtesy. They said: Messenger of Allah what is utmost kindness and courtesy? He replied: It is a day and a night. Hospitality extends for three days, and what is beyond that is charity on him; and he who believes in Allah and the Hereafter should say something good or keep quiet. (Abu Shuraih al-'Adwi (RA), Muslim, Vol III, p159, No. 48R1)

As guests, we should never abuse the generosity of our hostess by overstaying our welcome, as this may cause our hostess to commit bad deeds or say things she may later regret. This is made clear in the following hadith:

> The period of entertainment of a guest is three days, and utmost kindness and courtesy is for a day and a night. It is not permissible for a Muslim to stay with his brother until he makes him wrongdoing. They said: 'Messenger of Allah, how would he make him wrongdoing?' He replied: he stays with him so long that nothing is left with him to entertain him. (Abu Shuraih al-Khuza'i (RA), Muslim, Vol. III, p159. No.48R2)

We should also avoid causing annoyance to our hostess when visiting during the day or night or when accepting an invitation to dinner. If we state the time we expect to arrive and how long we intend to stay, we should keep within these time limits, unless our hostess asks us to arrive earlier or stay longer. This gives her time to plan and prepare provisions for entertaining and to delay or re-arrange normal family routines or social engagements. If we extend our visit without prior warning, we may disrupt whatever plans the sister had made for once we had left. Allah (SWT) had to remind the believing men to exercise this adab (courtesy) when visiting the Prophet (SAAS), as he was himself too shy to ask them to leave when they overstayed their welcome:

> **You who have iman! do not go into the Prophet's rooms except when you are invited to come and eat. Do not wait there while the food is being cooked. However, when you are called go in and when you have eaten disperse, not remaining there to chat with one another. Doing that causes annoyance to the Prophet though he is too reticent to tell you so. But Allah is not reticent with the truth...**
> **(Surat al-Ahzab 33: 53)**

Adab (courtesy) of Eating

> Whoever feeds a hungry Muslim will be fed by Allah from the fruits of the Garden; and whoever gives drink to a thirsty Muslim will be given pure wine to drink by Allah from the fountain of the Garden. (Abu Sa'id al-Khudri (RA), Abu Dawud, Vol. II, p441, No. 1678. Also at-Tirmidhi)

There are many blessings and rewards for feeding fellow Muslims. If food is prepared for one person it should be sufficient for two people. Similarly food prepared for two people should be sufficient for three people, and food for four people should be sufficient for five, six, or even eight people. ('Abd ar-Rahman ibn Abi Bakr (RA), Muslim, Vol. IIIB, p378, No. 2057. Jabir (RA), p380, No. 2059R3) Hence, if an unexpected guest pays a visit, we should also invite them to eat, as Allah (SWT) will bless the meeting and enhance the food's capacity. In addition to spiritual blessings, this act of kindness has many material blessings, as there is less wastage of food when more people are fed. (Commentary from Muslim, Vol. IIIB, p380, Footnote 3)

Before we eat we are advised to wash our hands. (Ibn 'Abbas (RA), Abu

Dawud, Vol. III, p1061, No. 3751) When the meal is served, everyone should gather together to eat at the same time to receive the full blessings of Allah (SWT). This includes family mealtimes. No one should begin eating until the host or hostess has given permission to do so. (Advice from Abu Dawud, Vol. III, p1063) There are several rulings concerning the prayer when it coincides with mealtimes. It is narrated in *Sahih Muslim* that the prayer is not valid when food has been served. Instead a Muslim should eat first (not hurriedly), then pray afterwards with a clear mind rather than think about food during the prayer. (al-Bukhari, Muslim, Ahmad) Other narrations on this matter are similar. If supper has been served at the time of the 'Isha prayer, the meal should be eaten first unhurriedly and the prayer performed afterwards. (Nafi', *Muwatta al-Imam Malik,* p412, No. 1754. Ibn 'Umar (RA), Abu Dawud, Vol. III, p1061, No. 3748. Anas ibn Malik (RA), al-Bukhari, Vol. 7, p269, No. 373) This ruling also applies for the Maghrib prayer. (Anas ibn Malik (RA), al-Bukhari, Vol. I, p362, No. 641) However, if meals are served at the time of other prayers they should only be delayed if a person is very hungry. If one can wait, prayer should be performed before the meal. (Jabir ibn 'Abdullah (RA), Abu Dawud, Vol. III, p1061, No. 3749. Footnotes 3195 & 3196)

> If supper is served and *iqamah* is pronounced [in the mosque] one should proceed with supper. (Ai'shah (RA), al-Bukhari, Vol. I, p362, No. 640)

When praying in a sister's house it is always good manners to ask her where to pray, so that she can direct you to the correct place. (Itban ibn Malik (RA), al-Bukhari, Vol. 1, p248, No. 416) It is bad manners and disrespectful to wander around someone's home without being invited. Children should also be taught to respect the host's privacy rather than run freely throughout every room in the house. If a room has been allocated for children to play, that is where they should stay. Similarly they should show respect for the possessions and belongings of their host. If there is damage to the property or a breakage, the sister should be offered a replacement or reimbursement. This is something the Prophet (SAAS) insisted upon when A'ishah (RA), smashed a food bowl belonging to one of his other wives. At this point, it is also important to mention the issue of parental responsibility. When we visit a fellow sister in her home, we should pay close attention to our role as mother and disciplinarian and ensure our children are well mannered and behaved. It is not an excuse to say that one is relaxing nor does it absolve one of one's Islamic duty and responsibility. If we lack consideration and show disrespect to our host or allow our children to be rude and unruly, we can expect very few, (if any) invitations to visit in the future.

The custom of the Prophet (SAAS) was that eating took place whilst sitting on the floor, rather than on chairs at the dining table. (at-Tirmidhi, Ch. XXVI, p125) The position we should assume for eating should be in an upright, sitting position, and not in reclining or leaning against something, unless we are ill or have some other legitimate excuse. (Abu Juhaifah (RA), al-Bukhari. Vol. 7, p234, No. 310. Abu Dawud, Vol. III, p1064, No. 3760) We should not eat lying on our stomach, ('Abdullah ibn 'Umar (RA), Abu Dawud, Vol. III, p1065, No. 3765) or sitting with our heels on our buttocks, (Jabir ibn Abdullah (RA), *Muwatta al-Imam Malik*, p285, No. 1648) or while standing. (Anas (RA), Muslim. Also *Riyad as-Salihin*, Vol. I, p300, No. 771)

Although it is permissible to drink Zamzam water while standing, (Ibn 'Abbas (RA), Muslim, Vol. IIIB, p358, No. 2027) some say that it is not permissible to drink ordinary water while standing (An-Nazzal (RA), al-Bukhari, Vol. 7, p357, No. 519 & 520) [although Imam Malik narrated that a number of Companions regarded that as acceptable (*Al-Muwatta*, Book 49, Number 49.8.13-49.8.16)]. However, even in the fomer position of some of the jurists, drinking while standing is not prohibited, but is merely disapproved according to them. If there is a legitimate reason for standing, it is permissible to do so, e.g. the ground is too wet or too dirty to sit upon and so forth. (Commentary taken from Muslim, Vol. IIIB, p358, Footnote 1 & 2)

If food is served and it appears unfamiliar, there is no harm if you enquire from your host about it, as the Prophet (SAAS) would rarely eat unfamiliar food unless it was described and named for him, (Khalid ibn al-Walid (RA), al-Bukhari, Vol. 7, Ch. 10, p230, No. 303). The host should respond well to this casual enquiry without feeling offended or insulted. It is strongly disapproved to question Muslim hosts about whether or not their food is halal

Before eating, we should always remember Allah (SWT) by invoking His name on the food, i.e. to say 'Bismillah' – 'In the name of Allah.' By doing this, we will receive His blessing and also prevent shaytan from eating with us. If we forget to mention Allah's name at the beginning of the meal, we should say 'In the name of Allah at the beginning and at the end of it.' If we forget to recite 'Bismillah', shaytan will share the food and take away the barakah (blessing). As a result we will be unable to satisfy our hunger and continue to overeat. (at-Tirmidhi, Ch. XXX, p134)

> When the companions of the Prophet (SAAS) said: "Apostle of Allah! We eat but we are not satisfied." He said: "Perhaps you eat separately." They replied: "Yes." He said: "If you gather together at your food and mention Allah's name, you will be blessed in it." (Washi ibn Harb on the authority of his father and his grandfather (RA), Abu Dawud, Vol. III, p1063, No. 3755)
>
> &
>
> When a man enters his house and mentions Allah's name on entering and on his food, shaytan says: "You have no place to spend the night and no evening meal," but when he enters without mentioning Allah's name on entering, shaytan says: "You have found a place to spend the night," and when he does not mention Allah's name at his food, he says: "You have found a place to spend the night and an evening meal." (Jabir ibn Abdullah (RA), Abu Dawud, Vol. III, p1063, No. 3756)
>
> &
>
> When one of you eats, he should mention Allah's name; if he forgets to mention Allah's name at the beginning, he should say: "In the name of Allah at the beginning and at the end of it." (A'ishah (RA), Abu Dawud, Vol. III, p1064, No. 3758. Also at-Tirmidhi)

There are additional blessings when eating together from one big plate rather than serving food on individual plates. It brings sisters closer together, it satisfies hunger and ultimately it saves on the washing up! To eat separately is also a sign of pride. Those who adopt this practice may nurse a sneaking hatred for the poor and an aversion for those who dine jointly from the same dish. (Commentary taken from at-Tirmidhi, Ch.XXVI, p125) The adab (courtesy) of eating from one plate is to eat what is directly in front of you and not to take portions from the far sides of the dish as they belong to other people. Food should not be eaten from the top or the middle of the plate, as Allah's blessings descend in these places. We should share blessings equally with others. When we eat, it is recommended to use the right hand rather than the left hand as shaytan eats and drinks with his left hand, ('Umar (RA), Abu

Dawud, Vol. III, p1065, Ch. 1423, No. 3767) and because the left hand is also used for cleansing one's private parts with water after using the toilet. It is also commendable to use three fingers while eating as the Prophet (SAAS) used to do, rather than use utensils such as a knives, forks or spoons. (Ka'b ibn Malik (RA), at-Tirmidhi, Ch. XXIV, p114)

> When one of you eats, he must not eat from the top of the dish, but should eat from the bottom, for the blessing descends from the top of it. (Ibn 'Abbas (RA), Abu Dawud, Vol. III, p1064, No. 3763)

&

> Blessings descend upon food in its middle, so eat from the edges of the vessel and do not eat from its middle. (Ibn 'Abbas (RA), at-Tirmidhi. Also Abu Dawud, and *Riyad as-Salihin*, Vol. I, p295, No. 744)

&

> 'Umar ibn Abi Salamah said: "I was a boy under the care of Allah's Messenger (SAW) and my hand used to go around the dish while I was eating. So Allah's Messenger (SAAS) said to me: 'Boy! Mention the name of Allah and eat with your right hand, and eat of the dish what is nearer to you.'" ('Umar ibn Abi Salamah (RA), al-Bukhari, Vol. 7, p221, No. 288)

If the food is not to our liking we should not let this be known to our hostess. Instead, we should respect her feelings, keep quiet and leave the food to one side on the plate, as the following hadiths state:

> Allah's Messenger (SAAS) never found fault with food served to him. If he liked anything, he ate it, and if he did not like it he left it,…and if he did not like it he kept silent. (Abu Hurairah (RA), Muslim, Vol. IIIB, p382, Nos. 2064 & 2064R3. Also in Abu Dawud, Vol. III, p1062, No. 3754)

Muslim parents are responsible for instilling these particular manners in their children, as they are often far too honest and can unintentionally hurt people's feelings. When a Muslim woman has worked hard to prepare a meal she should not be insulted or offended for her efforts. Instead, she should be shown sincere gratitude and appreciation.

On some social occasions, we may be expected to share a small amount of food with a large number of people. Although it might appear to be insufficient to satisfy hunger, Allah (SWT) will bless the food and enhance its capacity if we remember to say 'Bismillah'. In addition, a mumin eats with one intestine as opposed to a kafir who eats with seven intestines. (Abu Hurairah & Ibn 'Umar (RA), al-Bukhari, Vol. 7, p232, No. 306. Also Muslim, Vol. IIIB, p380, No. 2060) In other words, a muminah will always be satisfied with little and Allah (SWT) will make this easy for her.

Once we have finished eating, it is reommended to clean the dish with our fingers (if we ate with them) to receive the full blessings from Allah (SWT). We should afterwards wash our hands or at least wipe them with a handkerchief. If we wipe the bowl clean, Allah (SWT) will fill our bellies in the Hereafter. The bowl will also invoke for Divine pardon for us and say, "Just as you protected me from shaytan, may Allah, Most Holy also protect you from him." (at-Tirmidhi. Ch. XXXIII, p138) At-Tirmidhi explains that although it is difficult to comprehend how a soulless bowl can invoke Divine pardon, we should remember that all things in the heavens and the earth glorify Allah (SWT). He gives them the power of speech just as He causes the human tongue to speak. We should, therefore believe without question these prophetic statements rather than dismiss them.

> When one of you eats, he must not wipe his hand with a handkerchief until he licks it or gives it to someone to lick. (Ibn 'Abbas (RA), al-Bukhari, Vol. 7, p265, No. 366. Also Abu Dawud, Vol. III, p1081, No. 3838)

> &

> The Prophet (SAAS) commanded the licking of the fingers and the dish saying: "You do not know in which portion the blessing lies." (Jabir (RA), Muslim, Vol. IIIB, p361, No. 2033)

> &

> The Prophet (SAAS) used to eat with three fingers and not wipe his hand before licking it. (Ka'b ibn Malik (RA), Abu Dawud, Vol. III, p1081, No. 3839)

> &

> If anyone spends the night with grease on his hands which he has not washed away, he can only blame himself if trouble comes to him. (Abu Hurairah (RA), Abu Dawud, Vol. III, p1082, No. 3843)

At the end of the meal, we should always give thanks and praise to Allah (SWT) by saying *al-hamdullilah*. (Anas ibn Malik (RA), Muslim, Vol. IVB, p251, No. 2734) This is not only pleasing to Allah (SWT), but also the person who thanks Allah after eating is like someone who shows patience when fasting. (Abu Hurairah (RA), al-Bukhari, Vol. 7, p267, Ch. 57) It is also commendable to supplicate for the person who provided hospitality, food and drink, (Jabir ibn 'Abdullah & Anas (RA), Abu Dawud, Vol. III, p1082, No. 3844 & 3845) as the following hadiths reiterate:

> When the Apostle of Allah (SAAS) finished his food, he said: "Praise be to Allah Who has given us food and made us Muslims." (*al-hamdu lillaahi'l-ladhi at'amanaa wa saqaanaa wa ja'alanaa mina'l-Muslimeen*). (Abu Sa'id al-Khudri (RA), Abu Dawud, Vol. III, p1081, No. 3841)

> &

> Whenever the dining sheet of the Prophet (SAAS) was taken away (i.e. whenever he finished his meal), he used to say: "Praise be to Allah! Much good and blessed praise! O our Lord, we cannot compensate Your favour, nor can leave it, nor dispense with it." (*al-hamdulillaahi katheeran tayyiban mubaarakan feehi, ghaira makfiyyinn walaa muwadda'in walaa mustaghnan 'anhu Rabbana*). (Abu Umamah (RA), al-Bukhari, Vol. 7, p266, No. 368. Also *Riyad as-Salihin*, Vol. I, p291, No. 734)

Adab (courtesy) of Serving Drinks

When drinks are served to fellow sisters, we should ensure that everyone has been served first before we serve ourselves. (Abu Qatadah (RA), *Riyad as-Salihin*, Vol. I, p301, No. 773. Also at-Tirmidhi) It is also recommended for the younger generation to serve the older generation. (Anas (RA), al-Bukhari, Vol. 7, p361, Ch. 21, No. 526) Serving should go around to the right of the person first served, irrespective of the status and position of the person on the left. If we want to share our own drink with sisters, we should also first pass it to the sister on our right. If we want to share our drink with the sister on our left, we should first seek permission from the one on our right. She is then entitled to refuse our request if she so wishes. However she may want to sacrifice her turn to drink first to receive reward from Allah (SWT).

Allah's Messenger (SAAS) was given milk mixed with water, while

> a Bedouin was on his right and Abu Bakr was on his left. He drank of it and then gave it to the Bedouin and said, "The right, the right (first)." (Anas ibn Malik (RA), al-Bukhari, Vol. 7, p359, No. 523. Also Muslim, Vol. IIIB, p359, No. 2029)

&

> Allah's Messenger (SAAS) was given something to drink. He drank of it while on his right was a boy and on his left were some elderly people. He said to the boy: "May I give these (elderly) people first?" The boy said: "By Allah, Allah's Messenger! I will not give up my share from you to somebody else." On that Allah's Messenger (SAW) placed the cup in the hand of that boy. (Sahl ibn Sa'd (RA), al-Bukhari, Vol. 7, p360, No. 524)

Before we begin drinking, we should hold the glass in the right hand and say 'Bismillah.'

When drinking water, it is recommended (sunnah) to breath at least three times during the course of the drink and to take two or three mouthfuls (not one long one). In fact, many reports claim that it is forbidden to drink water in one breath, as it weakens the nerves and causes damage to the stomach and liver. (at-Tirmidhi, Ch. XLII, p173) It is permissible however, to drink with more than three breaths. Breathing-in between sips should take place outside the drinking vessel and not inside it and some say that at every pause we should say *'al-hamdulillah'*. All leftover water should be drunk, and once we have finished drinking, we should give thanks and praise to Allah (SWT).

> Anas used to breathe twice or thrice in the vessel (while drinking) and used to say that the Prophet (SAAS) used to take three breaths while drinking. (Thumamah ibn 'Abdullah (RA), al-Bukhari, Vol. 7, p365, No. 535)

&

> The Prophet (SAAS) had forbidden breathing into the vessel while drinking. (Abu Qatadah (RA), al-Bukhari, Vol. 7, p364, No. 534. Also Ibn 'Abbas (RA), Abu Dawud, Vol. III, p1054, Ch. 1401, No. 3719. Also at-Tirmidhi)

Invoking Blessings upon Someone Who Sneezes

Another obligation we have towards fellow Muslim sisters is to invoke blessings upon them when they sneeze. When they sneeze, they should say *al-hamdulillah* ('Praise belongs to Allah'). It is then our duty to offer *tashmit* in response to it, i.e. to say *yarhamuka'llah*:

> If any of you sneezes, he should say *'al-hamdulillah'* (Praise be to Allah), and his Muslim brother or companion should say to him *'yarhamuka'llah'* (may Allah bestow His mercy on you). When the latter says *'yarhamuka'llah'*, the former should say *'yahdikumu'llah wa-yuslih baalakum'* (May Allah guide you and improve your condition).' (Abu Hurairah (RA), al-Bukhari, Vol. 8, p157, No. 243)

> The *tashmit* i.e. to say *'yarhamuka'llah'* should only be offered if the Muslim woman who sneezes says *'al-hamdulillah'* first. If they forget to praise Allah (SWT), they should be reminded, and if they still refuse to say *'al-hamdulillah'*, the *tashmit* should not be offered.

Visiting the Sick

> The Prophet (SAAS) said: "Feed the hungry, visit the sick, and set free the captives. (Abu Musa al-Ash'ari (RA), al-Bukhari, Vol. 7, p375, No. 552)

Another Islamic obligation is to visit a fellow sister who is sick. We should offer her spiritual comfort and support and remind her of Allah's (SWT) closeness during this time. Visiting the sick also earns many rewards for the visitor.

> Whenever someone visits a sick person or a brother of his seeking the pleasure of Allah, an announcer calls out: "May you be happy, may your walking be blessed, and may you be awarded a dignified position in the Garden." (Abu Hurairah (RA), at-Tirmidhi. Also *Riyad as-Salihin*, Vol. I, p160, No. 362)

&

> For whoever visits a Muslim in the morning, seventy thousand angels will invoke the blessings for him till the evening. And if he visits him in the evening seventy thousand angels will invoke blessings on him till the morning, and for him is allotted an orchard of fruit trees in the Garden. ('Ali (RA), at-Tirmidhi. Also *Riyad as-Salihin*, Vol. II, p5, No. 899)

&

"If a Muslim visits his sick Muslim brother, he will stay among those engaged in picking fruit from the garden of Paradise, till he returns (from his visit)." Someone asked, "Messenger of Allah, what is *khurfat al-Jannah*?" He replied, "It is the picking of fruit." (Thauban (RA), Muslim. Also *Riyad as-Salihin*, Vol. II, p5, No. 898)

If we visit a Muslim woman who is sick, we should remind her of the rewards she will earn for being patient and the wrong actions she will expiate by her pain and suffering.

My Lord, God of mankind, Remover of affliction, cure, You are the Healer, there is no healer but You. A cure that leaves no sickness behind. (Anas ibn Malik (RA), al-Bukhari. Also *Riyad as-Salihin*, Vol. II, p6. No. 903)

&

You will have a double reward for being sick, and your wrong actions will be annulled as the leaves of a tree fall down. ('Abdullah ibn Mas'ud (RA), al-Bukhari, Vol. 7, p383, No. 565)

We should always make supplications to Allah (SWT) on behalf of the sister who is sick. Similarly we should ask her to pray for us as her prayers stand comparison to the prayers of angels. Allah (SWT) is also closer to those who are sick than those who are fit and healthy:

When you visit a sick person, ask him to pray for you since a sick person's prayers are like those of angels. ('Umar ibn al-Khattab (RA), Ibn Majah)

&

Allah (SWT) will say on the Day of Rising: "Son of Adam, I was sick but you did not visit Me." He will say: "My Lord; how could I visit You when You are the Lord of the worlds?" Thereupon He will say: "Didn't you know such and such slave of Mine was sick but you did not visit him and were you not aware that if you had visited him, you would have found Me by him?" (Abu Hurairah (RA), Muslim, Vol. IVA, p176, No. 2569)

Adab (courtesy) in Speech

Communication is important for maintaining strong ties of sisterhood, especially when accompanied by good manners, honesty, tact, diplomacy and discretion. However, these social skills are not always naturally inherent in our personalities. Instead we may need to learn them and instil them routinely into our everyday social discourse. Courtesy in speech is not only important for maintaining good relations, but it also places us in a better position in the Hereafter. The Prophet (SAAS) warned that the tongue, i.e. our speech, can either lead us to Garden or the Fire. Sometimes we may say things without realising the harm they cause. This is why we are advised to think before we speak and, if we cannot say anything nice, it is better to remain silent. If we control our evil speech during times of anger, jealousy, frustration or stress, Allah (SWT) will reward us in the Garden. Similarly, if we fail to restrain our speech, Allah (SWT) may punish us in the Grave and the Fire. If we fail to restrain our tongue during the month of Ramadan, Allah (SWT) may withhold our rewards and reject our fasts. (Ibn 'Abbas (RA), al-Bukhari, Vol. 1, p142, No. 217) This also applies to voluntary fasts.(Abu Hurairah (RA), al-Bukhari, Vol. 8, p53, No. 83)

> A slave speaks words whose repercussions he does not understand but because of which he sinks down in the Fire further than the distance between the east and the west. (Abu Hurairah (RA), Muslim, Vol. IVB, p383, No. 2988R1)
>
> &
>
> A slave of Allah may utter a word which pleases Allah without giving it much importance, and because of which Allah will raise him to degrees (of reward); a slave of Allah may utter a word carelessly which displeases Allah without thinking of its gravity and because of which he will be thrown into the Fire. (Abu Hurairah (RA), al-Bukhari, Vol. 8, p322, No. 485)

> &
> Whoever can guarantee what is between his two jaw bones and what is between his two legs (i.e. his tongue and his private parts), I guarantee him the Garden. (Sahl ibn Sa'd (RA), al-Bukhari, Vol. 8, p320, No. 481)

We should not only monitor our own speech but also the speech of our fellow sisters. If we fail to correct a sister who lies, swears, backbites or gossips, Allah (SWT) may not only judge her for her licentious comments but He may also judge us for listening to it. It is therefore, our duty as sisters-in-Islam to turn away from false or evil talk and adopt the following attitude:

> **When they hear worthless talk they turn away from it and say, "We have our actions and you have your actions. Peace be upon you. We do not desire the company of the ignorant." (Surat al-Qasas 28: 55)**

The following chapter aims to cover various issues regarding Islamic courtesy in speech.

Honesty in Speech

Speech is a powerful tool but it can often be used in the wrong way. It can be used to impress, oppress, deceive, intimidate or undermine. Speech can be beautified and words can be accentuated to influence or corrupt the attitudes and behaviours of others, i.e. in the case of lawyers and politicians who govern by laws other than those of Allah (SWT) and are governed by them. Lies can also be perpetrated to defend one's position or to govern and influence change. In Islam we should be particularly careful about the information we convey to others. It should always be righteous, honest and pure and free from lies, distortion or over exaggeration.

> The Prophet (SAAS) said: "Squandered are those who exaggerate in talk." He repeated it thrice. (Ibn Mas'ud (RA), Muslim. Also *Riyad as-Salihin*, Vol. II, p253, No. 1736)

Lying is only permitted in three cases in Islam. The first is with the intention of reconciliation between two people who are not on good terms. The second is in war and the third is when pleasing one's wife or husband, (Umm Kulthum (RA), Abu Dawud, Vol. III, p1371, No. 4903) although Imam Malik did not regard it as permissible for a couple to tell lies to each other. So in the case of creating harmony between people who are in a dispute with each other, lying is only permitted to improve relations rather than destroy them. Some people are better at lying than others. However the more we lie, the better we may become at it, until eventually we speak more lies than truths. Once this happens we can easily confuse reality with fantasy, and falsehood will become even more convincing than fact. Falsehood is a disease of the heart and can lead us to the Fire as the following hadiths re-iterate.

> Speak the truth for true speech points the way to good and good takes one to Garden; avoid falsehood, for falsehood leads the way to evil and evil takes one to the Fire. Have you not heard people saying: "Such and such spoke the truth and prospered and such and such spoke falsehood and suffered." ('Abdullah ibn Mas'ud (RA), *Muwatta al-Imam Malik,* p422, No. 1799)

> &

> When a man continually tells lies, a black spot is produced in his heart, till his whole heart is blackened and his name is written with Allah amongst the liars. ('Abdullah ibn Mas'ud (RA), *Muwatta al-Imam Malik,* p423, No. 1801)

The Prophet (SAAS) said that towards the end of time trustworthiness will disappear. Some of the contributing factors towards this unfortunate state of affairs are lies, carelessness in speech, making false promises and loose talk. While some people never say what they mean, there are others who never mean what they say. Some people make promises but are quick to break them, while others refuse to make any firm agreements or commitment. If Muslims fail to be decisive, honest or fair in their speech, it can lead to communication breakdown and poor relations in the community. This is why we are advised to emulate the Prophet (SAAS) in the way he spoke. Often he (SAAS) would remain silent and would not talk unless it was absolutely necessary. When he spoke, his words would be clear, simple and to the point. He was articulate, concise and precise and free from absurdity and ambiguity. He was never hot-tempered or impulsive in his speech or liable to humiliate, insult or offend. He was also courteous, polite and respectful and would avoid mentioning people by name when highlighting faults or correcting poor behaviour. Instead he would speak in general terms and refer in the plural rather than singular. Above all, he (SAAS) was truthful and honest. This is why he was called 'al-Ameen – the Trustworthy' and 'as-Sadiq – the Truthful.'

Whispering and Private Conversations

According to some, secrecy and confidential discussions between Muslims are not liked except in three cases:

1. When performing an act of sadaqah or kindness, i.e. giving material things or helping in moral, intellectual or spiritual matters.

2. When an unpleasant act of justice or correction has to be done.

3. To reconcile, quarrelling parties. (Commentary taken from 'Abdullah Yusuf Ali, *The Holy Qur'an*, p252, No.625, (Surah 4: 114))

It is however, acceptable in other cases with the permission of those present, for smaller groups to withdraw and talk confidentially together.

Muslims should always be pleasant in their manner and speech and think before opening their mouths, so as not to offend Allah (SWT) or upset the person to whom they are talking. If our speech is pleasant, there should be no need to whisper for fear or from shame of it being overheard by other people. Whispering is an act characteristic of shaytan. We are, therefore, advised not to do it. If we need to whisper or hold a private conversation, we should try to conduct it away from other sisters, or leave the discussion until a more appropriate time.

Conferring in secret is from Shaytan, to cause grief to those who have iman. (Surat al-Mujadilah 58: 10)

&

Whoever would believe in Allah and the Last Day then let him speak well or remain silent (i.e. abstain from dirty or evil talk, and think before talking). (Abu Shurayh al-Ka'bi (RA), *Muwatta al-Imam Malik,* 49.10.22. Also al-Bukhari, Vol. 8, p99, No. 157)

It is forbidden for two people to hold a private conversation when a third person is present without that person's permission, as it may cause offence or ill feeling. We should therefore prevent the sister from feeling paranoid or insecure and include her in all our conversations wherever possible. If there is a valid reason to talk secretly in a gathering, i.e. for personal advice or to enquire about a sister's welfare and there are more than three people present, it is permissible:

If you are three, two amongst you should not converse secretly between themselves to the exclusion of the other (third one), until some other people join him (and dispel his loneliness), for it may hurt his feelings. ('Abdullah ibn Mas'ud (RA), Muslim, Vol. IIIB, p447, No. 2184. Also al-Bukhari, Vol. 8, p204, No. 305)

Tact and Discretion

Allah disapproves of three things: He is angry with you for gossip, squandering property, and asking too many questions. (Abu Hurairah, al-Mughirah ibn Shu'bah, ash-Sha'bi and Warrad (RA), Muslim, Vol. IIIA, p151, No. 1715, p152, No. 593R1, 593R2, 593R3 & 593R4)

An important courtesy to remember in conversation is knowing when to talk and when to remain silent. This ruling applies in many social situations and for many good reasons. One particularly ill-mannered habit is to interrupt people when they are in mid-conversation. If there is good reason to interrupt and a suitable opportunity to do so and what you have to say is going to contribute well to the discussion, there is no harm in it, but if it is ill-thought out, meaningless or pointless, then it is better to keep quiet. The Prophet (SAAS) was very succinct and to the point when conversing and would rarely talk unless it was relevant and absolutely necessary. (Commentary taken from *Shamail at-Tirmidhi* by Imam Abu 'Isa at-Tirmidhi, Ch. XLIII, p180) This is something we should also consider in our own personal dialogues rather than talking merely for the sake of talking. Children should also be taught this courtesy and told not to interrupt adults when they are talking. (al-Bukhari, Vol. 8, p104, Ch. 89)

Persistent questioning is also disapproved in Islam, particularly when discussing knowledge of the deen. Although it is incumbent upon every Muslim to seek knowledge and gain correct understanding, we should try not to debate or investigate too deeply into matters that are either irrelevant or beyond the realms of ordinary human comprehension. Our knowledge may be very limited in certain areas, i.e. concerning the attributes of Allah (SWT), while other issues may not always be easy to explain in simple terms. Hence, we are advised not to question too deeply on less significant or complex issues as it may cause unnecessary confusion or disagreement between sisters. Instead, we should refer back to the Qur'an and Sunnah of the Prophet (SAAS) or seek proper advice from knowledgeable shaykhs and scholars.

Some conversations require a certain amount of tact and discretion. Although it is good to encourage one another to practice the Prophet's Sunnah (SAAS), there are certain practices that are better discussed on a general level rather than on a personal level. One example would be the obligatory act of shaving the pubic hairs (Ai'shah (RA), Muslim) or performing *ghusl* (bath). Some details may not be relevant or important to a discussion and therefore do not need to be mentioned. For example, when discussing one's agenda for the day it is not befitting to mention the need to perform *ghusl*, as this may reveal indulgence in marital relations the night before. This is a private matter and need not be disclosed. Tact and discretion should always be exercised when discussing sensitive or personal issues, as they may conjure up distasteful images and embarrass or offend the listener. Similarly, we should try not to enquire too deeply into a Muslim woman's private life, i.e. concerning their lifestyle before they embraced Islam, concerning their weekly wage/salary or the relationship they have with their husband and so on. A popular enquiry of many Muslim women concerns the desire to have (more) children. This is a personal matter between a Muslim woman and her husband, and is no one else's business. There are many reasons for not having children such as infertility, a husband's impotence or a doctor's orders because of a serious medical condition. Perhaps the sister is still recovering from a recent miscarriage. These are sensitive issues and particularly upsetting for the Muslim woman to discuss or broadcast to others. There are certain conversations that require sensitive treatment and should not be openly discussed. The range and nature of sensitive issues may differ from culture to culture and from person to person, but as a general rule we should always try to be more tactful and discreet in our social discussions.

Keeping Secrets

> When a man tells something and then departs, it is a trust. (Jabir ibn 'Abdullah (RA), Abu Dawud, Vol. III, p1357, No. 4850)

A sister's private life is her own business. If she feels comfortable enough to disclose certain information in her conversations, we should be trusted not to disclose it to other people. Confidentiality should be maintained at all times no matter how trivial the subject matter may seem. There are only three particular instances when confidentiality can be broken, which are as follows:

> Meetings are confidential except three: those for the purpose of

shedding blood unlawfully, or committing fornication, or acquiring property unjustly. (Jabir ibn 'Abdullah (RA), Abu Dawud, Vol. III, p1357, No. 4851)

If we promise not to disclose certain information in our conversations, we must keep to our word. If we break our trust, Allah (SWT) may hold us accountable for it on the Day of Judgement.

> Fulfil your contracts. Contracts will be asked about. (Surat al-Isra 15: 34)

Even if we disclose information without the sister's knowledge, Allah is All-Knowing and All-Aware, and He (SWT) may seek retribution on her behalf either in this life or on the Day of Judgement.

They try to conceal themselves from people, but they cannot conceal themselves from Allah. He is with them when they spend the night saying things which are not pleasing to Him. Allah encompasses everything they do. (Surat an-Nisa 4: 107)

&

Four are the qualities which, if found in a person, make him a hypocrite; if he possesses one of them, he possesses one characteristic of hypocrisy till he abandons it. These are: When he is entrusted with something, he betrays the trust; when he talks, he lies; when he makes a covenant, he acts treacherously and when he falls out, he deviates from the path of truth (reviles). ('Abdullah ibn 'Amr ibn al-'As (RA), agreed upon. Also *Riyad as-Salihin*, Vol. I, p541, No. 690)

&

On the Day of Judgement, the worst of the people in Allah's sight, will be the man who consorts with his wife and then publishes her secret. (Abu Sa'id al-Khudri (RA), Muslim. Also *Riyad as-Salihin*, Vol. I, p537, No. 685)

Although the last hadith is with respect to a man concerning his wife, it also applies to a woman concerning her husband. Not only is it disrespectful and distasteful to disclose personal and intimate details about one's marriage relationship, it may also cause embarrassment and offence to the sister who has to hear it. In addition, the Prophet (SAAS) stated that a man or a woman who disclose their intimate bedroom secrets are like male and female shaytans who meet on the road and satisfy their sexual desires while people look on. (Abu Hurairah (RA), by the compilers of the *Sunan*. See *The Lawful and the Prohibited in Islam* by Yusuf al-Qaradawi, I.I.F.S.O., p197,) If a Muslim woman discloses personal details concerning her marital relationship, she should be corrected for her misdemeanours in speech and her private life should still remain confidential.

Gossip and Idle Talk

Idle talk and gossip are condemned in Islam, as these acts weaken iman and diminish good deeds. They also corrupt the mind and harden the heart. We are therefore, advised to keep away from sisters who spread lies and mischief with their idle gossip, and we should refrain from listening to it or doing the same.

> **It is the muminun who are successful: those who are humble in their salat; those who turn away from worthless talk... (Surat al-Mu'minun 23: 3)**
>
> &
>
> The Prophet (SAAS) said: "Do not speak much without remembering Allah, for much talk without remembrance of Allah produces hardness of heart, and the one who is farthest from Allah is he who has a hard heart." (Ibn 'Umar (RA), at-Tirmidhi)

Too much talk reduces our fear of Allah (SWT), and tempts us to commit greater wrong actions, i.e. to exaggerate, backbite, slander etc. Allah (SWT) is witness to everything we do and everything we say. He assigns two angels to every man and woman to record all their words and deeds. One angel records all our good deeds and good speech while the other one records all our bad deeds and bad speech. If we want to be successful on the Day of Judgement it is in our own best interests to speak well about people or remain silent:

> **He does not utter a single word, without a watcher by him, pen in hand! (Surah Qaf 50: 18)**
>
> &
>
> 'Whoever has iman in Allah and the Last Day then let him speak well or remain silent.' (Abu Hurairah (RA), Abu Dawud, Vol. III, p1425, No. 5135)

Gossip is forbidden in Islam, as it may involve falsehood and harm the honour and dignity of the person discussed. It also weakens the ties of sisterhood. A gossip derives pleasure in discussing the private lives of other people and creates excitement and intrigue from their pain and misery. They also exaggerate certain details for mere shock or entertainment value. Among the tales they tell are lies, assumptions, faultfinding and slander. A gossip is quick to judge and condemn other people for their faults and weaknesses yet will often overlook their own.

> The Prophet (SAAS) forbade gossip (*qeela* and *qaala,* i.e. someone said, and he said, …etc). (Warrad (RA), al-Bukhari, Vol. 8, p319, No. 480)

> &

> Do not express pleasure at the misfortune of a brother lest Allah bestows mercy upon him and involves you in misfortune. (Wathilah ibn al-Asqa' (RA), at-Tirmidhi. Also *Riyad as-Salihin,* Vol. II, p208, No.1577)

Although it is highly disliked to discuss the affairs of another Muslim in a way which would be injurious to him or displeasing to him, Imam an-Nawawi states that it may be justified to inform on another Muslim in the following situations:

1. If a man commits murder, rape or other serious crimes, and another man knows of it,

2. If a man becomes the victim of highhandedness at the hands of a tyrant,

3. If a man knows that important information has not been given to someone who needs it, and they may suffer loss because of it, i.e. a wicked man intending to marry a woman, (Commentary taken from Muslim, Vol. IVA, p191, Footnote 2. Also Muslim, Vol. IA, p69, Footnote 2)

4. To seek help to stop a practice which may be against Islam,

5. To caution Muslims against the evil consequences of some mischief,

6. To seek a ruling (*fatwa*) on a specific topic from a qualified person in authority,

7. If someone indulges in wrong practices openly, i.e. publicly

drinking alcohol, cruel treatment of people, expropriation of their property, and imposition and collection of illegal taxes with cruelty. (*Riyadh as-Salihin*, Arabic – English, Vol. II, p739)

It may be possible before discussing these matters with others to approach the person directly and ask them to cease their wrong actions. However, if that and other means fail, then the above allow one to discuss his or her wrong actions with others. Although the examples mentioned above permit us to reveal the true nature and character of a wrongdoing Muslim, it is important that our intentions for doing so are honest and pure, and not to deliberately cause harm or damage to the individual's reputation. The benefits of revealing a Muslim's faults must outweigh the harm of concealing a Muslim's faults. The information we convey must be factually correct and based upon reliable evidence and credible witnesses and not on the basis of hearsay. The Prophet (SAAS) warned about the dangers of transmitting information without verifying its authenticity or truthfulness. This is why we should be careful not to broadcast hearsay. If we hear something about a fellow Muslim, we should ascertain whether or not it is true. If it is true, it may be broadcast to others if it is absolutely necessary, i.e. for the seven reasons already mentioned.

> It is sufficient falsehood for a man to relate everything he hears. (Abu Hurairah (RA), Abu Dawud, Vol. III, p1389, No. 4975)

While some people are very open about their private lives, others may be a little more reserved. Hence privacy should be respected at all times. If we hear something concerning a fellow sister, we should keep it confidential, especially if it is of a sensitive or personal nature. Gossiping and telling tales is a grave wrong action in Islam, especially if it is done with the intention of creating dissension among Muslims. A *Qattat* (gossip), a person who does just this, will be severely punished in the Fire.

> A *Qattat* (tale bearer) shall not enter the Garden. (Hudhaifah (RA), al-Bukhari, Vol. 8, p52, No. 82. Also Muslim, Vol. IA, p69, No. 105)

When a gossip spreads a malicious rumour, it may damage the good character of its victim. If the rumour is true, the gossip will be judged for backbiting. If the rumour is not true, the gossip will be judged for slander, which is even worse!

Backbiting

The Prophet (SAAS) defined backbiting as the following:

> The Prophet (SAAS) said: "Do you know what backbiting is? To mention about your brother that which he hates." They said: "Even if what we say about our brother is true?" He said: "If it is true what you say of him, then that is backbiting, and if it is not true what you say of him, then you have slandered him." (Abu Hurairah (RA), Abu Dawud, Vol. III, p1358, No. 4856)

&

> Backbiting is describing the state of a man in such a manner that, if he should hear it, it would seem repugnant to him.

Backbiters very rarely consider the harm that is caused by their comments. When they discuss and criticise people, they will often identify certain flaws in a person's character. It makes little difference whether these faults or weaknesses are large or small or whether they are the only faults the person has against an otherwise good character. Criticisms and faultfinding can seriously damage a person's good reputation and can also tarnish the way other people perceive their character too. The Prophet (SAAS) said: "None of my companions should convey to me something indecent regarding another because I desire to meet everyone of you with a clear heart." (Ibn Mas'ud (RA), Abu Dawud, at-Tirmidhi. Also *Riyad as-Salihin*, Vol. II, p191, No. 1536) We should also adopt this attitude to prevent clouding our own judgements of one another. A habitual backbiter fails to see anything good in people. Instead she focuses on people's flaws and weaknesses and exaggerates them. Ironically a backbiter usually has more faults than those of her victims. She may suffer from many personal insecurities and deficiencies and harbour suspicion, intolerance, jealousy and resentment, yet secretly wish to be like her victims in appearance, character, skills, abilities, achievements and so on. Backbiters also like to assume the motives behind a person's behaviour, but by doing so they merely reveal their own suspicious and bad motives. Unfortunately, human judgement is not accurate and actions can easily be misinterpreted. The backbiter may then be guilty of spreading lies and slander.

Only Allah (SWT) has the authority to judge our intentions, as only He knows what our hearts conceal. Only He (SWT) knows whether actions are due to deliberate wrong action and transgression or mere human error. Instead of being suspicious and quick to find faults in others, we should try to make more excuses for our fellow sisters-in-Islam and learn to be more forgiving. If Allah (SWT) can forgive us for all our wrong actions, then we should be willing to forgive other Muslim women for theirs.

> **You who have iman! avoid most suspicion. Indeed some suspicion is a crime. And do not spy and do not backbite one another. Would any of you like to eat his brother's dead flesh? No, you would hate it. (Surat al-Hujurat 49: 12)**

&

> Beware of suspicion (about others), as suspicion is the falsest talk, and do not spy upon one another, and do not listen to the evil talk of people about others' affairs, and do not have enmity with one another, but be brothers. (Abu Hurairah (RA), al-Bukhari, Vol. 8, p59, No. 92)

'Isa (AS) [Jesus] also said:

> Do not look at the wrong actions of people as if you were lords. Look at your wrong actions as if you were slaves. Some people are afflicted by wrong action and some people are protected from it. Be merciful to the people of affliction and praise Allah for His protection. (Reported by *Muwatta al-Imam Malik,* p420, No. 1791)

The punishment for backbiting will be experienced in both the grave and the Fire:

> The backbiter will never enter the Garden. (Hudhaifah (RA), agreed upon. *Riyad as-Salihin*, Vol. II, p190, No. 1536. Also Muslim, Vol. IA, p69, No. 105)

&

> The Prophet (SAAS) said: "When I was taken up to Heaven (i.e. *al-Mi'raj*), I passed by some people who were scratching their faces and chests with their nails which were made of copper. I asked Jibril, 'Who are these people?' and he replied, 'These are the people who used to eat the flesh of other men (who were given to backbiting) by attacking their honour and respect.'"

(Anas ibn Malik (RA), Abu Dawud, Vol. III, p1359, No. 4860)

Unfortunately backbiting is a trait inherent in all of us and we often say more than we should during conversations, especially those of an interesting or scandalous variety. Sometimes we backbite people and do not even realise we are doing it. This is why it is important not to become too relaxed when we speak. Instead, we should monitor what we say and exercise more self-restraint. If we do not, we will backbite, gossip and slander more and more until eventually it becomes a habit that is hard to break.

Furthermore, if we see something in a sister that is not to our liking, we should tactfully bring it to her attention rather than broadcast her misdemeanours to the rest of the community. She then has an opportunity to turn to Allah (SWT) from her wrongdoings and correct herself in the future. Allah (SWT) will then reward her for amending her ways and reward us for guiding her to more right-acting Islamic behaviour. It will also conceal the wrong action from other people and prevent them from incurring wrong actions with their own backbiting, slander and gossip.

> Some say that Allah the Blessed, the Exalted, will not punish the many for the wrong action of the few. However, when the objectionable action is committed openly, then they all deserve to be punished. (A saying of 'Umar ibn 'Abd al-'Aziz (RA), *Muwatta al-Imam Malik,* p423, No. 1806)

As mentioned before if we hear sisters backbiting, we should tactfully discourage them. We should then defend the Muslim woman who was criticised and make excuses for her wherever possible. If the sisters persist in their vain talk and refuse to stop we should withdraw from their company, as Allah (SWT) has described the behaviour of the muminun:

When they hear worthless talk they turn away from it. (Surat al-Qasas 28: 55)

Slander

> The Prophet (SAAS) said: "Should I inform you that slandering, is a tale-carrying which creates dissension amongst people, and he (SAAS) further said: "A person tells the truth until he is recorded as truthful, and he tells lies until he is recorded as a liar." ('Abdullah ibn Mas'ud (RA), Muslim, Vol. IVA, p191, No. 2606)

A slanderer is a person who says something about another person that is not true. As mentioned before, the Prophet (SAAS) warned that slandering is worse than backbiting, as it spreads lies and damages the honour and reputation of innocent people. He (SAAS) also warned that if someone is falsely accused of unscrupulous or corrupt behaviour, the accusation returns to the one who utters it, i.e. the slanderer.

> When any Muslim accuses another Muslim of debauchery or kufr, the reproach rebounds upon the one who utters it if that person is not deserving. (Abu Dharr (RA), al-Bukhari. Also *Riyad as-Salihin*, Vol. II, p203, No. 1560)

A slanderer who spreads lies about other people will receive a painful punishment in this life and the next. (Surat an-Nur 24: 19) On the Day of Judgement, Allah (SWT) will restrain slanderers on the bridge overhanging the Fire, and He will keep them there until their victims have been cleared of all false accusations and allegations. (Mu'adh ibn Anas (RA), Abu Dawud, Vol. III, p1360, No. 4865) As Muslims, we should avoid slander and defend fellow sisters from it in their absence. The Prophet (SAAS) said if a Muslim deserts another Muslim when his respect is violated and his honour aspersed, Allah will desert him in a place where he wishes His help. However if a Muslim helps another Muslim when his honour is aspersed and his respect violated, Allah will help him in a place where he wishes His help. (Jabir ibn 'Abdullah and Abu Talhah ibn Sahl al-Ansari (RA), Abu Dawud, Vol. III, p1360, No. 8466) Allah will also send an angel to guard his flesh on the Day of Rising from the fire of Jahannam. (Mu'adh ibn Anas (RA), Abu Dawud, Vol. III, p1360, No. 4865)

> The Prophet (SAAS) said: "Whoever defends the honour of his brother in his absence will receive protection from the Fire." (Asma bint Yazid (RA), Ahmad and also at-Tirmidhi)

&

> The mumin is a mirror for the mumin , and the mumin is the brother of the mumin. He safeguards his property for him and defends him in his absence. (Abu Hurairah (RA), Abu Dawud, Vol. III, p1370, No. 4900)

In the narration by at-Tirmidhi, the Prophet (SAAS) was also reported to say, "so if he sees any fault in him, he should wipe it away from him." A good practising Muslim woman should see her own faults in another

Muslim woman as she sees herself in the mirror. She should, therefore, make it her duty to wipe out the faults of herself and those of her fellow sister.

Muslims who spread lies about other Muslims will be severely punished in the grave and the Fire, especially if it is with the intention of sowing dissension. Many hadiths relate to the punishment of a liar. On the Day of Rising a liar will have a hooked piece of iron like a meat cleaver inserted into one side of the jaw and it will rip through the flesh to the back of the neck. The same will be done to the other side of the jaw. When both jaws are restored, this painful procedure will be repeated over and over again. (Ibn 'Umar, (RA) al-Bukhari. Also *Riyad as-Salihin*, Vol. II, p194)

> The Prophet (SAAS) passed by two graves and said: "Both of these people in the grave are being tortured and they are not being tortured for a major wrong action. This one used not to save himself from being soiled with his urine, and the other used to go about with calumnies (among people to rouse hostilities, e.g. one goes to a person and tells him such and such evil things)." (Ibn 'Abbas (RA), al-Bukhari, Vol. 8, p49, No. 78)

Seeking Forgiveness for Backbiting and Slander

If our evil comments damage the good reputation of a fellow sister and whether she finds out or not, we should ask for her forgiveness. If we do not, Allah (SWT) will either transfer our good deeds to her on the Day of Judgement or transfer her bad deeds on to us.

> Whoever has oppressed another person concerning his reputation or anything else, he should beg him to forgive him before the Day of Rising as there will be no money to compensate for wrong deeds. Instead, if he has good deeds, they will be taken from him according to the wrong he has caused, and if he has no good deeds, the bad actions of the wronged person will be loaded on him. (Abu Hurairah (RA), al-Bukhari, Vol. 3, p377, No. 629)

If an apology is offered, it should be accepted with good grace. If the sister does not accept the apology then she will incur the wrong action:

Correct and courteous words accompanied by forgiveness

are better than sadaqa followed by insulting words. (Surat al-Baqarah 2: 263)

&

If a Muslim brother apologises to another Muslim, and the latter does not accept his apology, then against him will be the same wrong action as is against the person who collects a tax which is not due. (Ibn Majah)

If we develop reputations for gossiping or backbiting, Muslim women may start to avoid us to safeguard their own honour and reputations. We will then hold the worst position in Allah's estimation on the Day of Rising:

The one who will have the worst position in Allah's estimation on the Day of Resurrection will be the one whom people left alone for fear of his ribaldry. (A'ishah (RA), Muslim, Vol. IVA, p184, No. 2591. Also Abu Dawud, Vol. III, p1342, No. 4373)

&

'The worst people are those whom people desert or leave in order to save themselves from their dirty language or from their wrongdoing. (A'ishah (RA), al-Bukhari, Vol. 8, p50, No. 80)

&

Among the most evil of people is the one with whom people are cautious because of his evil. (Malik (RA), *Muwatta al-Imam Malik*, p377, No. 1610)

Concealing Faults

In Islam it is forbidden to expose our own faults (wrong actions). It is also forbidden to seek out and expose the faults of fellow Muslims. If we reveal the faults of a Muslim, Allah (SWT) will expose our faults and humiliate us in this life and the next.

The Prophet (SAAS) said: "Every one of my followers will be forgiven except those who explore their wrongdoings in the open. ...it is an impudent for a man to commit a deed at night, and Allah keeps it secret but he gets up at dawn and says: 'So and so, I have committed such and such acts last night.' He slept in the night and Allah veiled him but at dawn he removes the veil of Allah by himself." (Abu Hurairah (RA), Muslim, Vol. IVB, p384, No. 2990)

&

The Prophet (SAAS) said, "People who believe by your tongues, yet iman does not enter your hearts, do not backbite Muslims, and do not search for other people's faults, for if anyone searches for their faults, Allah will search for his fault, and if Allah searches for the fault of anyone, He disgraces him in his house. (Abu Barzah al-Aslami (RA), Abu Dawud, Vol. III, p1359, No. 4862)

In Islam it is seriously disliked to discuss, judge or criticise the behaviour and actions of a fellow Muslim as it leads to suspicion and weakens ties in the community. Suspicion is the whispering of shaytan and can lead to backbiting and slander and create dissension among people. Instead, we should harbour good thoughts about one another and conceal rather than reveal one another's flaws and misdemeanours. If we conceal the faults of a fellow Muslim, Allah (SWT) will conceal our faults on the Day of Judgement. (Abu ad-Darda (RA), at-Tirmidhi)

To harbour good thoughts is a part of well conducted worship. (Abu Hurairah (RA), Abu Dawud, Vol. III, p1389, No. 4975)

&

Beware of suspicion. Suspicion is the most untrue speech. Do not spy and do not eavesdrop. Do not compete with each other and do not envy each other and do not hate each other and do not shun each other. Be slaves of Allah, brothers. (Abu Hurairah (RA), *Muwatta al-Imam Malik,* p379, No. 1621. Also Abu Dawud Vol. III, p1370, No. 4899)

&

If you find faults with a Muslim, you will create dissension among them. (Ibn Mas'ud (RA), Abu Dawud. Also *Riyad as-Salihin*, Vol. II, p207, No. 1571)

Furthermore, we should try to make excuses for a sister's poor behaviour to protect her honour and good reputation.

...and there is no one who loves to accept an excuse more than Allah... (Sa'd ibn 'Ubadah (RA), al-Bukhari, Vol 9, p378, No. 512. Also Muslim, Vol. 2, p782, No. 3572)

As mentioned before, exceptions to the rule for concealing faults apply in the following situations:

1) In a court of law,

2) When obtaining an opinion concerning a proposal for marriage,

3) Concerning a person representing any public office,

4) When seeking a fatwa or advice regarding the behaviour of another person,

5) Warning people of innovators and wrongdoers, but only in relation to actions done openly not secretly,

With the exception of the circumstances mentioned above, we should always try to forgive rather than condemn a fellow Muslim for wrongdoings. The following ayat and ahadith provide good incentives for concealing faults and for showing forgiveness:

They should rather pardon and overlook. Would you not love Allah to forgive you? (Surat an-Nur 24: 22)

&

He who sees something which should be kept hidden and conceals it will be like the one who has brought to life a girl buried alive. ('Uqbah ibn 'Amir (RA), Abu Dawud, Vol. III, p1362, No. 4873)

&

Allah will not show mercy to those who do not show mercy to others. (Jarir ibn 'Abdullah (RA), al-Bukhari and Muslim. Also *Riyad as-Salihin*, Vol. I, p113, No. 227. Also 'Abdullah ibn Amr (RA), Abu Dawud, Vol. III, p1375, No. 4923)

It is wrong to criticise the character of a fellow Muslim without just cause. We should never accuse a sister of wrong action, immoral behaviour or refer to her as a kafirah, unless she openly declares herself as such. No one is perfect and we are all liable to make mistakes and fall into error at times. If we are unable to overlook the faults of a fellow sister, how can we expect other Muslim women to do the same for us?

If a man says to his Muslim brother, 'O kafir!' it is true about one of them. ('Abdullah ibn 'Umar (RA), *Muwatta al-Imam Malik*, p419, No. 1784)

&

> Let no man accuse another of unrighteousness or kufr, lest, should he be mistaken, that he himself, is as he says. (Abu Hurairah (RA), al-Bukhari)
>
> &
>
> When you hear a man saying the people have perished, it will be he himself who will suffer most. (Abu Hurairah (RA), *Muwatta al-Imam Malik*, p419, No. 1785)

It is hard enough to live harmoniously in this society among the kuffar, without causing divisions between sisters as well. We should therefore, learn to control our emotions and be more forgiving, put unnecessary differences aside and encourage one another to maintain strong ties of sisterhood for the sake of Allah (SWT).

Being Two-Faced

People who are two-faced deceive people by their false character, by showing one face to one group of people and another face to another group of people. This is one of the most abhorrent failings of a Muslim's character as it hides other evil traits such as hypocrisy, deceit, insincerity, cowardice, and selfishness. Two-faced people are liars, who believe they can fool people with their pretence. But in reality, they only fool themselves. This type of person is the most contemptible creature in the eyes of Allah, (Commentary taken from Muslim, Vol. IVA, p190, Footnote 2) and will eventually be despised by her own family and friends. If her devious character is exposed in this life, she risks losing all her close network of friends and other sincere relationships. However, the greatest loss will be in the Hereafter, when Allah (SWT) will expose and humiliate her for her despicable acts of deception.

> The worst in the sight of Allah on the Day of Rising will be two-faced people who appear to some people with one face and to other people with another face. (Abu Hurairah (RA), al-Bukhari, Vol. 8, p53, No. 84)
>
> &
>
> He who is two-faced in this world will have two tongues of fire on the Day of Rising. ('Ammar (RA), Abu Dawud, Vol. III, p1358, No. 4855)

Envy

Islam only permits envy in two cases. The first is envy of a Muslim who is blessed with wealth and spends it for the sake of Allah (SWT). The second is envy of a Muslim who has good Islamic knowledge which he learns, studies and teaches to others. (Ibn Mas'ud (RA), agreed upon. Also *Riyad as-Salihin*, Vol. I, p228, No. 544)

Envy is an emotion originating from shaytan and is strictly forbidden in Islam. It is a very powerful, negative, and all-consuming emotion. It hardens the heart and can ruin the good deeds of even the best of the muminun. It not only destroys the self, but it can also destroy everything else that is good in our lives. It can destroy families, friendships, marriages and even professional working relationships. But worst of all, it can have a detrimental affect on the relationship we have with our own Creator. Muslims, who harbour ill feeling and jealousy towards other Muslims, build a closer relationship with shaytan rather than Allah (SWT), and will find their good deeds diminished by bad deeds on the Day of Judgement.

> Beware of envy because it consumes the virtues just as fire consumes fuel (grass or wood). (Abu Hurairah (RA), Abu Dawud, Vol. III, p1366, No. 4885)

To curb feelings of jealousy and envy, we are advised not to look at the lives of those who are better off materially. Instead we should look to those who are worse off in terms of material wealth, health and so on. This will enable us to be more grateful for Allah's blessings and favours rather than bitter and resentful for the things we do not and may never have.

> Look at those who are less fortunate than you and do not look at those who are more fortunate than you, for this will enable you to appreciate better the favours of Allah. It will keep you from despising Allah's favours to you. (Abu Hurairah (RA), Muslim. Also *Riyad as-Salihin*, Vol. I, p201, No. 467)

Allah (SWT) blesses us all in one way or another. We should therefore thank him for all His kind favours and be pleased for the favours He bestows upon others.

> **Or do they in fact envy other people for the bounty Allah has granted them? (Surat an-Nisa 4: 54)**

Quarrelling

Quarrelling and bad feeling amongst sisters should be avoided, as it weakens iman and increases bad deeds. In addition, the one who quarrels is the most hated person in the sight of Allah (SWT):

> The most hateful person in the sight of Allah is the most quarrelsome person. (A'ishah (RA), al-Bukhari, Vol. 3, p381, No. 637)

When there is hatred, jealousy or spite, shaytan will heighten these feelings by whispering and inventing stories. Eventually we will begin to imagine things that haven't actually been said or done. As time elapses ill feeling can increase and hatred may become so intense it will be too difficult to restore good relations. It may even provoke verbal or physical abuse and the cutting of ties. This is why we are commanded in Islam to refrain from cursing and abusing one another.

> Some people asked Allah's Messenger (SAAS) "Whose Islam is the best?" He replied, "One who avoids harming the Muslims with his tongue and hands." (Abu Musa (RA), al-Bukhari, Vol. I, p19, No. 10)

&

> Abusing a Muslim is debauchery and fighting him is kufr. ('Abdullah ibn Mas'ud (RA), Muslim, Vol. I, A, p50, No. 64. Also al-Bukhari, Vol. 8, p43, No. 70)

&

> The Messenger of Allah (SAAS) said on the Farewell Pilgrimage: "Woe to you, distress to you! Don't turn back as kuffar after me by striking the necks of another. ('Abdullah ibn 'Umar (RA), Muslim, Vol. IA, p51, No. 66R1)

In Islam, it is forbidden to curse or invoke curses on another person, (Samurah ibn Jundub (RA), Abu Dawud, Vol. III, p1367, No. 4888) as we do not know when Allah (SAW) may grant our request. (Jabir ibn 'Abdullah, Abu Dawud, Vol. 1, Ch. 513, No.1527) Sometimes we may do or say something in the heat of the moment, not realising the consequences of our actions or speech. Although we may wish the worst for someone in a fit of rage, we may regret it once embittered emotions have subsided. However, by then it may be too late, as Allah (SWT) may have already granted our request. Alternatively, we may say something of which the person is not deserving and cause the curse to rebound upon ourselves. (Abu'd-Darda (RA), Abu Dawud, Vol. III, p1367, No. 4887) Cursing a mumin is such a grave wrong action that it is equivalent to the crime of murder. (Abu Zaid ibn Thabit ibn Dahhak (RA), agreed upon, *Riyad as-Salihin*, Vol. II, p200, No. 1551) It will also prevent us from interceding or witnessing on the Day of Rising. (Abu'd-Darda (RA), Abu Dawud, Vol. III, p1367, No. 4889)

If two sisters quarrel, the one who first began the abuse will incur a wrong action, unless the one who is abused retaliates and transgresses the limits set by Allah (SAW). Although retaliation is permitted in the case of self-defence, the sister should not inflict an injury greater than she received. After retaliation, the score is even and the dispute should be settled. However, if the first sister abuses again and transgresses the limits set by Allah (SWT), the second Muslim woman is then entitled to Allah's protection in spite of her own faults, as Allah is the One who forgives our wrong actions again and again. (Commentary taken from the *Holy Qur'an*, translated by 'Abdullah Yusuf Ali, Surah 22:60, Footnote 2840)

> **And if anyone inflicts an injury the same as the one done to him and then is again oppressed, Allah will come to his aid. Allah is All-Pardoning, Ever-Forgiving. (Surat al-Hajj 22: 58)**

&

> When two persons indulge in hurling abuse upon one another, the first is the wrongdoer as long as the oppressed does not transgress the limits. (Abu Hurairah (RA), Muslim, Vol. IVA, p183, No.2587. Also Abu Dawud, Vol. III, p1363, No. 4876)

Although it is permitted for the abused person to retaliate in self-defence, it is actually recommended not to do so. If we remain calm and forgiving and do not return the abuse, Allah will reward us for trying to pacify the situation. He will also elevate us in respect and esteem among people. The Prophet (SAAS) also praised the one who shows endurance when harmed. (Commentary taken from Muslim, Vol. IV,A, p183, Footnote 1) Allah also says:

> **But if people do defend themselves when they are wronged, nothing can be held against them for doing that. There are**

only grounds against those who wrong people and act as tyrants in the earth without any right to do so. Such people will have a painful punishment. But if someone is steadfast and forgives, that is the most resolute course to follow. (Surat ash-Shura: 38-40)

&

Being patient when harmed by others. (see Chapter 70 on *Adab* – Courtesy, al-Bukhari, Vol. 8)

&

The steadfast will be paid their wages in full without any reckoning. (Surat az-Zumar 39: 11)

&

And the slave who pardons, Allah adds to his respect, and the one who shows humility, Allah elevates him in the estimation of people. (Abu Hurairah (RA), Muslim, Vol. IVA, p183, No. 2588)

&

The Prophet (SAAS) said: "Happy is the man who avoids dissension; but how fine is the man who is afflicted and shows endurance. (Al-Miqdad ibn al-Aswad (RA), Abu Dawud, Vol. III, p1185, No. 4250)

If a sister harms us and we choose not to retaliate, we should supplicate to Allah (SWT) as He always responds to those who have suffered abuse, oppression or wrongdoing. This also includes those who have incurred other forms of unnecessary injury such as slander and defamation of character, physical and mental abuse, etc.

> Three supplications are answered, there being no doubt about them; that of a father, that of a traveller, and that of one who has been wronged. (Abu Hurairah (RA), Abu Dawud, Vol. 1, Ch. 515, No. 1531. It is not necessary that a person oppressed or wronged is a pious Muslim for the supplication to be answered, for he may be a profligate or rather kafir (Footnote 861))

If we hurt a Muslim woman's feelings unintentionally, we are advised to make supplications for them. This is something the Prophet (SAAS) used to do when he felt he had abused or upset someone:

> The Prophet (SAAS) said: "O Allah! If I should hurt somebody, let

> it be a means of purification and mercy for him." (al-Bukhari, Vol.8, p 247, Ch. 34)

> &

> The Prophet (SAAS) said: "O Allah! If I should ever abuse a mumin, please let that be a means of bringing him near to You on the Day of Rising." (Abu Hurairah (RA), al-Bukhari, Vol. 8, p247, No. 372)

In Islam, the best reason for retaliation should be that it is for Allah's sake and to defend the deen of Islam. However, it is not permissible for Muslims, men or women, to dispute excessively about knowledge of the deen from their own opinions. Heated debates on the Islamic Shari'ah (Law) and 'aqidah (principles of iman) should be avoided at all times. Instead we are recommended to seek advice from learned scholars and Islamic jurists.

> The Messenger of Allah (SAAS) did not take revenge for himself unless the limits of Allah were violated. Then he took revenge for it for Allah. (A'ishah (RA), *Muwatta al-Imam Malik*, p376, No. 1608. Also al-Bukhari, Vol. 8, p557, No. 836)

> &

> Upon seeing two men arguing with each other about an ayah of the Qur'an, the Prophet (SAAS) was clearly angered saying: "The people before you were ruined because of their disputation about the Book," he also warned: "The most despicable amongst men to Allah is that vehement disputer." (A'ishah (RA), Muslim, Vol. IVB, p222, No. 2666 & 2668)

Shaytan will always try to incite hatred and enmity between Muslims. (Jabir (RA), Muslim, Vol. IVB, p301, No. 2813) It is, therefore, important to restrain our tongues and our hands, and suppress bad emotions and desires such as anger, bitterness, jealousy or spite. Failure to do so gives victory to shaytan and earns Allah's displeasure. It will also increase our bad deeds on the Day of Judgement. If we want to save ourselves from the Fire and attain entry into the Garden we should treat others, as we would want to be treated in return. ('Abdullah ibn 'Amr ibn al-'As (RA), Muslim. Also *Riyad as-Salihin*, Vol. II, p204, No.1566)

> The strong man is not the one who wrestles well but the strong man is one who controls himself when he is in a rage. (Abu

Hurairah (RA), Muslim, Vol IV A, p193, No. 2609)

Controlling Anger

The way we can control feelings of anger is to supplicate to Allah with the words *"a'udhu billahi mina'sh-shaitani'r-rajim* – I seek refuge with Allah from the accursed shaytan". We should also change our position i.e. from standing to sitting or from sitting to lying down. We can also perform wudu to extinguish feelings of anger. These techniques for controlling anger are recommended in the three following hadiths:

> Two men reviled each other in the presence of the Prophet (SAAS) and one of them became excessively angry so much so that I thought that his nose will break up on the excess of anger. The Prophet (SAAS) said: "I know a phrase, which, if he repeated, he could get rid of this angry feeling." They asked: "What is it Messenger of Allah? He replied: He should say: "I seek refuge with Allah from the accursed shaytan." (Mu'adh ibn Jabal (RA), Abu Dawud, Vol. III, p1340, No. 4762)

> &

> The Messenger of Allah (SAAS) said to us: "When one of you becomes angry while standing, he should sit down. If the anger leaves him well and good, otherwise he should lie down." (Abu Dharr (RA), Abu Dawud, Vol. III, P1340, No. 4764)

> &

> The Messenger of Allah (SAAS) said: "Anger comes from shaytan, shaytan was created of fire, and fire is extinguished only by water, so when one of you becomes angry, he should perform wudu. ('Atiyyah (RA), Abu Dawud, Vol. III, p1340, No. 4766)

If we restrain our tempers during times of anger we will earn high rewards, as it will help to prevent dissension and division between Muslims. Reward will also be earned on the Day of Rising when Allah (SWT) will call us over the heads of all creatures and ask us to choose any of the bright and wide-eyed maidens we wish. (Sahl ibn Mu'adh (RA), Abu Dawud, Vol. III, p1339, No. 4759) Obviously this is with respect to a man who suppresses his anger. Only Allah (SWT) knows the equivalent reward for a woman who shows the same amount of self-control. However, suffice it to say it will be worthwhile, as Allah (SWT) is never unjust and He has promised we can have whatever our hearts desire in the Garden.

Cutting Ties with Sisters

The most virtuous forms of worship are keeping relationships and avoiding enmity towards people. Muslims should never sever ties of kinship or friendship as it can increase tension and lead to further division in the community. It is not permissible for Muslims to dispute to the point where they no longer speak. Similarly disputing Muslims should not ignore one another if they pass on the street or at a talk or special function. Instead, they should be civil and polite and greet one another. Both Muslims are equally responsible for bringing about reconciliation, irrespective of who was in the wrong. The better of the two is the one who offers the greeting/salaams first. (Abu Ayyub al-Ansari (RA) Muslim, Vol. IV, p172, No. 2560) The other sister should then respond to the greeting. If she fails to do so, she will incur the wrong action and be judged accordingly. In addition, Allah (SWT) does not forgive the wrong actions of the two parties until they reconcile:

> The gates of the Garden are opened twice a week – on Mondays and Thursdays. Allah then forgives every believing slave who does not associate anything with Him, except the one who feels malice towards one of his Muslim brothers. Instead, Allah says, "Leave these two until they reconcile." (Abu Hurairah (RA), Abu Dawud, Vol. III, p1369, No. 4898)

&

> Do not hate each other, nor be envious of each other, nor harbour enmity for each other, and become brother and slaves of Allah. It is not lawful for a Muslim that he should estrange his relations with his brother beyond three days. (Anas ibn Malik (RA), al-Bukhari Vol 8, p62, Muslim, Vol. IV, p171, No. 2559)

&

> It is not permissible for a mumin to keep apart from another mumin for more than three days. After three days have elapsed and he happens to meet him, he should greet him. If he answers the greeting, then both will share the rewards (*ajr*), and if he does not answer the greeting, he will bear the wrong action, and the one who greeted will be innocent of the wrong action

of severing relations. (Abu Hurairah (RA), Abu Dawud, Vol. III, p1368, No. 4894)

The last hadith allows three days to let bad feelings subside. After this time, it is the responsibility of both Muslims to restore the relationship and return to as normal a routine as possible.

If quarrelling sisters refuse to reconcile, it may be necessary for others to intervene to aid and encourage communication and restore good relations. All Muslims are responsible for encouraging peace between disputing Muslims even if it becomes so serious that there is no other way to do it and one has to lie. In a case such as this, lying would not be considered a wrong action, as it is good to reconcile people who are on bad terms. (Humaid ibn 'Abd ar-Rahman (RA), Abu Dawud, Vol. III, p1370, No. 4902) Encouraging peace between disputing Muslims is also considered more excellent in degree than fasting, prayer and giving sadaqah. (Abu'd-Darda (RA), Abu Dawud, Vol. III, p1370, No. 4901)

The muminun are brothers, so make peace between your brothers and have taqwa of Allah so that hopefully you will gain mercy. (Surat al-Hujurat 49: 10)

During a dispute a sister may oppress another Muslim woman by refusing to communicate. This denies the opportunity for the latter to express her version of events or encourage reconciliation. If slander is involved the sister will be oppressed even further as she may not be able to repair the damage caused to her reputation. As a result, she may lose self-confidence and respect and become isolated from the rest of the community. Oppression is forbidden in Islam, as the following hadith states:

> A Muslim is a brother of another Muslim, so he should not oppress him, nor should he hand him over to an oppressor. Whoever fulfils the needs of his brother, Allah will fulfil his needs; whoever brings his (Muslim) brother out of discomfort, Allah will bring him out of the discomforts of the Day of Rising, and whoever screens a Muslim, Allah will screen him on the Day of Rising. ('Abdullah ibn 'Umar (RA), al-Bukhari, Vol. 3, p373, No.622)

Although disputing Muslims should not keep apart for more than three days, they are permitted to keep apart for the sake of Allah. For instance, if children disobey Allah (SWT) and their parents' instructions, they can keep apart from them for a time as an admonition. Similarly a husband can keep apart from his wife for a period of time if she disobeys Allah and disrespects his instructions in matters of the deen. The Prophet (SAAS) kept apart from some of his wives for forty days, for demanding more provision and worldly comforts. He did not want them to become interested in the superficial comforts of this world. Ibn 'Umar (RA) kept apart from his son until he died. Hence the Prophet (SAAS) prohibited a Muslim from keeping apart in the case of dispute and petty quarrelling, but permitted it for the sake of Allah (SWT) to defend the deen of Islam. (Commentary taken from Abu Dawud, Vol. III, p1369, Footnote, 4274 & 4278) This is a sensitive and very serious issue and one that requires further understanding. Please seek advice from reputable scholars before disassociating with people for the sake of Allah (SWT). Alternatively refer to other relevant books on the subject. This is not a practice to be taken light-heartedly.

Conclusion

Islam unites all Muslims in peace and harmony and binds them together by their iman and sense of humanity. However, the strength of the Muslim Ummah (community) is dependant upon the actions and behaviour of each of its members. The amount of love, compassion and concern each Muslim has towards others also plays an important role. Allah (SWT) commands us to fulfil certain rights, roles, duties and responsibilities towards our fellow sisters-in-Islam and to ensure all their basic needs and requirements are met. Allah (SWT) provides guidance for social behaviour that encourages good relations and will reward us for fulfilling our social duties and obligations. He will also reward us for simple acts of kinship and for displaying good manners and social courtesy. If we fail to observe these duties and obligations we will not only cause further division within the Muslim community but also earn the displeasure and punishment of Allah (SWT). It is therefore in our own best interests to adhere to Allah's divine guidance and the Prophet's Sunnah (SAAS) if we want to achieve success in this life and the next. May Allah (SWT) continue to guide us and help us improve in our everyday Islamic duty and obligations.